Good Housekeeping
COOKIES!

FAVORITE RECIPES FOR DROPPED,
ROLLED & SHAPED COOKIES

Clockwise from top: Pennsylvania-Dutch Brownies (page 148), Almond Slices (page 116), Honey Cookies (page 90), Pfeffernusse (page 70)

Good Housekeeping

COOKIES!

FAVORITE RECIPES FOR DROPPED, ROLLED & SHAPED COOKIES

HEARST BOOKS

A division of Sterling Publishing Co., Inc.

New York / London

www.sterlingpublishing.com

GOOD HOUSEKEEPING

Rosemary Ellis
Editor in Chief

Sara Lyle
Lifestyle Editor

Susan Westmoreland
Food Director

Samantha B. Cassetty, M.S., R.D.
Nutrition Director

Sharon Franke
Food Appliances Director

BOOK DESIGN by Memo Productions
Photography Credits on page 174.

Library of Congress Cataloging-in-Publication Data is available.

10 9 8 7 6 5 4 3 2 1

The Good Housekeeping Cookbook Seal guarantees that the recipes in this cookbook meet the strict standards of the Good Housekeeping Research Institute. The Institute has been a source of reliable information and a consumer advocate since 1900, and established its seal of approval in 1909. Every recipe has been triple-tested for ease, reliability, and great taste.

Published by Hearst Books
A division of Sterling Publishing Co., Inc.
387 Park Avenue South, New York, NY 10016

Good Housekeeping is a registered trademark of Hearst Communications, Inc.

www.goodhousekeeping.com

For information about custom editions, special sales, premium and corporate purchases, please contact Sterling Special Sales Department at 800-805-5489 or specialsales@sterlingpublishing.com.

Distributed in Canada by Sterling Publishing c/o Canadian Manda Group, 165 Dufferin Street Toronto, Ontario, Canada M6K 3H6

Distributed in Australia by Capricorn Link (Australia) Pty. Ltd.
P.O. Box 704, Windsor, NSW 2756 Australia

Manufactured in China

Sterling ISBN 978-1-58816-826-9

CONTENTS

Chocolate-Chunk Cookies (page 20), Sour-Cream Cookies (page 38),
Chewy Peanut Butter Cookies (page 26)

FOREWORD

Welcome to *Good Housekeeping Cookies!* Whether you are an experienced cookie baker or a novice preparing to bake your first batch, you are about to discover how simple and satisfying cookie baking can be. Just the aroma of cookies baking, whether they are plain or

 fancy, trendy or traditional, brings out a smile from anyone who passes by. In our test kitchens at *Good Housekeeping*, whenever we bake cookies, the rest of the magazine staff stops in more frequently than usual. We always reward them with a taste of whatever we are baking, and in return many of them have shared with us their family's favorite cookie recipes.

The recipes that follow have been selected from the many hundreds in the *Good Housekeeping* collection. Most were developed in our test kitchens, some have come from staff, and some from readers, but all have been triple tested (and staff tasted), so we know they are good. We hope that the time you spend baking recipes from *Cookies!* will leave you with many warm and wonderful memories.

SUSAN WESTMORELAND
Food Director, *Good Housekeeping*

Gingerbread Cutouts (page 138)

PERFECT COOKIES EVERY TIME

What smells better than a batch of cookies hot from the oven? Better yet is when they turn out just the way you want them—moist and chewy, or light and crispy—never burned or dried out. And getting it right is easy if you follow the step-by-step directions that come with every recipe and use the ingredients called for.

Most cookies don't require any fancy equipment. However, there are a few essential baking utensils that can make the difference between a cookie that tastes just so-so and one that makes folks say, Wow—these are great! So before you start baking, it's a good idea to make sure you have the right equipment on hand and that you're using the best ingredients.

Measure By Measure

The primary reason cookies don't turn out quite right is usually failure to measure ingredients properly. More than any other form of cooking, baking requires very precise measurements. Even though it worked for Grandma, don't use coffee or tea cups, or tableware teaspoons and tablespoons for measuring. Ideally, you should have:

- a set of standard dry measuring cups
- a set of standard measuring spoons
- a spatula for leveling them
- 1-cup, 2-cup, and 4-cup glass measures for liquids.

The Right Cookie Sheets

High-quality cookie sheets and baking pans are the second most important secret to baking perfect cookies. You should use heavy-gauge metal sheets and pans with a dull finish—we recommend aluminum. These double-thick insulated cookie sheets and baking pans will help prevent your cookies

Standard dry measuring cups and spoons (made of metal), and 1-, 2-, and 4-cup glass measuring cups

from getting extra-dark bottoms. Avoid dark cookie sheets—they also can blacken the bottoms of cookies because they absorb more heat. If your cookie sheets are old and discolored, you can line them with foil to help deflect the heat.

Size is important too. Cookie sheets should be at least 2 inches smaller in length and width than your oven so that air can circulate freely around them. So measure your oven before you buy new cookie sheets. If possible buy rimless sheets, or those with only one or two edges turned. They will also help air to circulate around the cookies.

Mixing It Up

While a lot of cookie batters can be stirred up with whatever spoon is on hand, the right equipment makes this task easier, particularly if your recipe calls for chopping a lot of nuts or doing a lot of mixing. You should have:

- a stand mixer or hand beater
- a food processor or mini processor
- a set of mixing bowls: small, medium, and large
- several wooden spoons

Timing Is Everything

One of the most common mistakes is not timing the baking properly, which results in burned or underdone cookies. Fortunately, this problem is easily avoided. Buy a good oven thermometer and check it closely to make sure your oven is at the correct temperature before you start baking. It's also wise to start checking your cookies a couple of minutes before they're supposed to be done. So get a kitchen timer and set it a few minutes early.

Cool Ideas

To remove the hot cookie sheets from the oven safely, you will need two sturdy pot holders. Use a toothpick to test bar cookies for doneness. The bars are done when a toothpick inserted 2 inches from edges comes out almost clean. Next, you'll need racks on which to set the baking sheets while the cookies cool and a wide metal spatula to transfer the cookies from the sheet. Never set a hot sheet on the counter.

Into the Cookie Jar

When the cookies are cool, you'll want to store them so they stay nice and crisp—or chewy, as the case may be. You can use either a tin or a jar, as long as it has a tight-fitting cover.

Specialty Cookie Equipment

Baking supply shops have enough cookie-making tools to fill all the shelves in your kitchen, and it would be fun to have them all. But you don't need them. You can bake every recipe in this book with just a few additional utensils and you probably already own a lot of them:

- cookie cutters of various shapes
- cookie press for molded cookies
- cookie scoops
- grater
- juicer
- parchment paper
- pastry bag and large tips
- pastry brush
- pastry cloth
- pastry wheel
- rolling pin and pin cover
- ruler
- wire whisk
- yeast thermometer

The Ingredients of Success

Baking is a precise art. To ensure that your cookies will taste delicious and have just the right texture, it is important to use the exact ingredients called for and handle them properly.

- **Butter or margarine?** While either one may be used for many cookie recipes, for the best flavor and texture, use butter. If you prefer to use margarine, make sure it contains 80 percent fat. Don't substitute light margarine or vegetable-oil spreads for stick margarine, and don't use whipped butter, either. Those products contain more water than standard sticks and won't work in cookies unless the recipes have been formulated especially for them.

To soften butter or margarine, let it stand, wrapped on a counter or unwrapped in a mixing bowl, at room temperature for an hour. You can speed up the process by cutting it into small pieces first. It's best not to soften butter or margarine in the microwave. The microwave can melt some areas, which can hurt the cookies' texture.

To grease cookie sheets, your best bet is vegetable shortening. Avoid both butter, which browns, and vegetable oil, which leaves a gummy residue on baking pans. Grease cookie sheets only when a recipe directs you to. Some cookies have a high fat content, so greasing isn't necessary.

• **The type of flour is important.** Most cookie recipes call for all-purpose flour. Occasionally, a cookie recipe will call for cake flour, which is higher in starch and will produce a more tender cookie. Cake and all-purpose flours are not interchangeable, so read your recipe carefully. In either case, make sure the flour you are using is not self-rising.

• **Baking soda is a leavening agent**—it makes cookies rise. Keep the box or tin tightly closed in a cool, dry place so the baking soda stays very active. For best results, replace it after six months if you haven't used it up.

• **Baking powder is a premeasured mixture** of baking soda and an acid. (It takes twice as much baking powder as baking soda to leaven a product.) Again, keep baking powder tightly closed in a cool, dry place and for best results, replace it after six months.

The Way to Measure

To get the same results every time you make a recipe, it is important to use standard measuring equipment and to measure carefully.

• **Always** use standard measuring spoons to measure both liquid and dry ingredients. For convenience, measure the dry ingredients first.

• **Never** use dry-ingredient cups to measure liquid ingredients or liquid-ingredient cups to measure dry ingredients.

• **Always** measure ingredients over waxed paper or into an empty bowl but never over your bowl of already measured ingredients—just in case there is a spill.

• **Liquids.** Use clear glass measuring cups. Place the cup on a level surface and bend down so that your eyes are in line with the marks on the cup.

- **Dry ingredients.** To measure flour and other dry ingredients that tend to pack down in the storage container, stir and then spoon them into a standard dry-ingredient measuring cup. Level the top surface with a spatula or back of a knife, scraping off the excess into a bowl.

Stir the flour and spoon it into a standard dry measuring cup to keep it from packing.

Level the top of the dry measure by passing a metal spatula over the top to remove excess.

- **Sugar.** Just scoop or pour granulated into a dry-ingredient measuring cup then level with the back of a knife. Confectioners' sugar should be sifted before measuring to break up clumps. Lightly spoon it into the measuring cup and then level. To measure brown sugar, pack it into the measuring cup and then level.
- **Butter, vegetable shortening, and margarine.** Tablespoons are marked on the wrapper, so you can just cut off the desired amount using a knife.
- **Syrup, honey, and other sticky ingredients.** Lightly oil the cup first and the ingredient will pour right out without sticking to the cup.

Now perfectly equipped, with the right ingredients on hand, you're ready to bake fabulous cookies!

DECORATING: A SHORT AND SWEET GUIDE

Like cheerfully wrapped packages, cutout cookies with bright trimmings are always inviting. A basic recipe for Ornamental Frosting follows, along with suggestions for tools to apply it. But if you don't have time to pipe on frostings or paint intricate designs, here are some other fun techniques. These methods work their magic in minutes and are fun to do with kids.

Before-Baking Brushes

Egg-Yolk Wash: Beat 1 large egg yolk with ¼ teaspoon water. Divide beaten egg among a few small cups and tint each with food coloring.

Milk Paint: Tint a couple tablespoons of canned evaporated milk with food coloring for an old-fashioned glazed look.

After-Baking Flourishes

Sugar Coating: Boil 1 cup light corn syrup for 1 minute, stirring. Brush syrup on the cookie, then dust with colored sugar crystals or sprinkles, or press on candy decors. Or, fill small bowls with trimmings and dip the brushed side of the cookie into a bowl to decorate.

Fast Frosting: Whisk 1½ cups confectioners' sugar with 1 to 2 tablespoons milk until blended; tint the mixture with the desired food coloring and brush it on.

Marbling: Brush on an even coat of Ornamental Frosting (opposite). With the tip of a small paintbrush, drop dots of another frosting color on top. Using a toothpick, drag the edges of the colored dots through the base frosting in a swirling motion to create fanciful designs.

Candy Land: Frost cookies with store-bought frosting, then press on chocolate chips, miniature marshmallows, gumdrops, gummy candy, and so on, to create tempting treats.

Hot Chocolate: Melt white or dark chocolate; pour it into a small zip-tight plastic bag. Snip ⅛ inch off a bottom corner of the bag (this is your writing tip). Drizzle the chocolate over baked cookies. Variations: Write names, draw simple shapes such as hearts and stars, or use the chocolate as glue to anchor decors and candies. Allow 2 hours or more to dry.

ORNAMENTAL FROSTING

This fluffy frosting is perfect for decorating holiday cookies. The recipe originally called for three raw egg whites, and you can use them if pasteurized eggs are sold in your area. We prefer meringue powder, which is sterilized and now available at many supermarkets and baking supply stores.

ACTIVE TIME: 5 MINUTES
MAKES: ABOUT 3 CUPS

1   PACKAGE (16 OUNCES) CONFECTIONERS' SUGAR

3   TABLESPOONS MERINGUE POWDER

⅓   CUP WARM WATER

ASSORTED FOOD COLORINGS (OPTIONAL)

1   In large bowl, with mixer at medium speed, beat confectioners' sugar, meringue powder, and water until mixture is stiff and knife drawn through leaves path, about 5 minutes.

2   If desired, tint frosting with food colorings. Keep tightly covered to prevent drying out. With small metal spatula, artist's paintbrushes, or decorating bags with small plain tips, decorate cookies with frosting. (You may need to thin frosting with a little warm water to obtain ideal spreading or piping consistency.)

EACH TABLESPOON: ABOUT 39 CALORIES | 0G PROTEIN | 10G CARBOHYDRATE | 0G TOTAL FAT (0G SATURATED) | 0G FIBER | 0MG CHOLESTEROL | 2MG SODIUM

DROP COOKIES

Quick to mix up, fun to spoon onto cookie sheets, and easy to bake, drop cookies offer almost immediate gratification. No wonder they are often the first cookies young bakers prepare by themselves—chocolate chip cookies in particular. In this chapter you'll find all-time classics, regional specialties, international favorites, plus the latest treats—there's something here for every cookie lover.

Although drop cookies are a snap to make, you will get even better results if you keep these simple tips in mind.

- **To promote even baking,** make sure each ball of raw cookie dough is the same size. You can use a measuring spoon to scoop up equal portions of dough for each cookie or invest in a cookie scoop that will measure the dough as well as push it out onto the sheet.

- **For perfectly shaped cookies,** leave enough space between the drops of dough so that the cookies don't spread together during baking. Unless the recipe directs otherwise, 2 inches apart is a good standard.

- **To prevent the dough from spreading,** cool the sheets between batches. Spreading dough causes the cookies to run together and creates a thinner cookie that is more likely to burn. Simply run first lukewarm and then cool water over the back of each sheet between batches.

- **To prevent cookies from sticking to the sheet,** always check greased sheets to see if they need regreasing between batches.

Clockwise from top: Chewy Peanut Butter Cookies (page 26), Chocolate Chip Cookies (page 18), Chewy Molasses-Spice Cookies (page 37)

CHOCOLATE CHIP COOKIES

Here's America's favorite cookie. You might want to bake a double batch, because they will disappear in no time. For a wonderfully decadent variation, try the White Chocolate–Macadamia Cookies below.

ACTIVE TIME: 15 MINUTES · **BAKE TIME:** 10 MINUTES PER BATCH
MAKES: 36 COOKIES

1¼ CUPS ALL-PURPOSE FLOUR	¾ CUP GRANULATED SUGAR
½ TEASPOON BAKING SODA	2 LARGE EGGS
½ TEASPOON SALT	1½ TEASPOONS VANILLA EXTRACT
½ CUP BUTTER OR MARGARINE (1 STICK), SOFTENED	1 PACKAGE (6 OUNCES) SEMISWEET CHOCOLATE CHIPS (1 CUP)
½ CUP PACKED LIGHT BROWN SUGAR	2 CUPS PECANS (8 OUNCES), CHOPPED (OPTIONAL)

1 Preheat oven to 375°F. In small bowl, combine flour, baking soda, and salt.
2 In large bowl, with mixer at medium speed, beat butter and brown and granulated sugars until light and fluffy. Beat in eggs and vanilla until well combined. Reduce speed to low; beat in flour mixture just until blended. With wooden spoon, stir in chocolate chips and pecans, if using.
3 Drop dough by rounded tablespoons, 2 inches apart, on two ungreased cookie sheets. Bake until golden around edges, 10 to 12 minutes, rotating cookie sheets between upper and lower oven racks halfway through baking. With wide metal spatula, transfer cookies to wire racks to cool completely.
4 Repeat with remaining dough.

EACH COOKIE: ABOUT 80 CALORIES | 1G PROTEIN | 11G CARBOHYDRATE | 4G TOTAL FAT (2G SATURATED) | 1G FIBER | 13MG CHOLESTEROL | 79MG SODIUM

WHITE CHOCOLATE–MACADAMIA COOKIES

Prepare as directed but substitute **¾ cup white baking chips** for **semisweet chocolate chips** and **1 cup chopped macadamia nuts (5 ounces)** for pecans.

EACH COOKIE: ABOUT 110 CALORIES | 1G PROTEIN | 11G CARBOHYDRATE | 7G TOTAL FAT (3G SATURATED) | 0.5G FIBER | 13MG CHOLESTEROL | 84MG SODIUM

WHITE CHOCOLATE–CHERRY MACADAMIA JUMBOS

Chock-full of cherries, chocolate, and macadamia nuts, just one of these cookies is a dessert by itself. But when you sandwich a scoop of your favorite ice cream between two, it's a party waiting to happen.

ACTIVE TIME: 15 MINUTES · **BAKE TIME:** 15 MINUTES PER BATCH
MAKES: 24 COOKIES

2½ CUPS ALL-PURPOSE FLOUR

¾ CUP BUTTER OR MARGARINE (1½ STICKS), SOFTENED

¾ CUP GRANULATED SUGAR

⅓ CUP PACKED DARK BROWN SUGAR

3 TABLESPOONS CORN SYRUP

2 TEASPOONS VANILLA EXTRACT

1 TEASPOON BAKING SODA

1 TEASPOON SALT

2 LARGE EGGS

12 SQUARES (12 OUNCES) WHITE CHOCOLATE, COARSELY CHOPPED

1 JAR (6½ OUNCES) MACADAMIA NUTS, CHOPPED (ABOUT 1⅓ CUPS)

1½ CUPS DRIED TART CHERRIES

1 Preheat oven to 325°F. In large bowl, with mixer at medium speed, beat flour, butter, granulated and brown sugars, corn syrup, vanilla, baking soda, salt, and eggs until blended, occasionally scraping bowl with rubber spatula. With spoon, stir in white chocolate, nuts, and dried cherries.

2 Drop dough by slightly rounded ¼ cups, 3 inches apart, on ungreased large cookie sheet. Bake until lightly browned, 15 to 17 minutes. With wide metal spatula, transfer cookies to wire rack to cool.

3 Repeat with remaining dough.

EACH JUMBO COOKIE: ABOUT 310 CALORIES | 4G PROTEIN | 37G CARBOHYDRATE | 16G TOTAL FAT (7G SATURATED) | 3G FIBER | 37MG CHOLESTEROL | 275MG SODIUM

CHOCOLATE-CHUNK COOKIES

A cookie jar just isn't well stocked unless there's something chocolate in it. This cookie is perfect for people who like a dose of decadence in their afternoon snack.

ACTIVE TIME: 30 MINUTES · **BAKE TIME:** 10 MINUTES PER BATCH
MAKES: 36 COOKIES

2½ CUPS ALL-PURPOSE FLOUR	½ CUP GRANULATED SUGAR
1 TEASPOON BAKING SODA	2 TEASPOONS VANILLA EXTRACT
½ TEASPOON SALT	2 LARGE EGGS
1 CUP BUTTER OR MARGARINE (2 STICKS), SOFTENED	8 SQUARES (8 OUNCES) BITTERSWEET CHOCOLATE, CUT INTO ½-INCH CHUNKS
1 CUP PACKED BROWN SUGAR	1 CUP WALNUTS (4 OUNCES), COARSELY CHOPPED

1 Preheat oven to 375°F. Grease large cookie sheet.

2 In medium bowl, combine flour, baking soda, and salt.

3 In large bowl, with mixer at medium speed, beat butter and brown and granulated sugars until creamy, occasionally scraping bowl with rubber spatula. Beat in vanilla, then eggs, one at a time, beating well after each addition. At low speed, gradually add flour mixture; beat just until blended, occasionally scraping bowl. With wooden spoon, stir in chocolate and walnuts.

4 Drop cookies by heaping tablespoons, 2 inches apart, on prepared cookie sheet. Flatten with a small metal spatula as shown opposite. Bake until lightly browned, 10 to 11 minutes. With wide metal spatula, transfer cookies to wire rack to cool.

5 Repeat with remaining dough.

EACH COOKIE: ABOUT 170 CALORIES | 3G PROTEIN | 19G CARBOHYDRATE | 10G TOTAL FAT (5G SATURATED) | 1G FIBER | 26MG CHOLESTEROL | 130MG SODIUM

FLATTENING STIFF COOKIE DOUGH

A stiff cookie dough will bake more evenly if flattened slightly with a small metal spatula after it is dropped onto the cookie sheet.

CHOCOLATE WOWS

The name says it all! Three kinds of chocolate plus pecans make a spectacular cookie.

ACTIVE TIME: 20 MINUTES · **BAKE TIME:** 13 MINUTES PER BATCH
MAKES: 48 COOKIES

⅓ CUP ALL-PURPOSE FLOUR

¼ CUP UNSWEETENED COCOA

1 TEASPOON BAKING POWDER

¼ TEASPOON SALT

6 SQUARES (6 OUNCES) SEMISWEET CHOCOLATE, CHOPPED

½ CUP BUTTER OR MARGARINE (1 STICK)

2 LARGE EGGS

¾ CUP SUGAR

1½ TEASPOONS VANILLA EXTRACT

2 CUPS PECANS (8 OUNCES), CHOPPED

1 PACKAGE (6 OUNCES) SEMISWEET CHOCOLATE CHIPS (1 CUP)

1 Preheat oven to 325°F. Grease two large cookie sheets. In small bowl, combine flour, cocoa, baking powder, and salt.

2 In heavy 2-quart saucepan, melt chocolate and butter over low heat, stirring frequently, until smooth. Remove from heat and cool.

3 In large bowl, with mixer at medium speed, beat eggs and sugar until light and lemon colored, about 2 minutes, frequently scraping bowl with rubber spatula. Reduce speed to low. Add cooled chocolate mixture, flour mixture, and vanilla; beat just until blended. Increase speed to medium; beat 2 minutes. With wooden spoon, stir in pecans and chocolate chips.

4 Drop batter by rounded teaspoons, 2 inches apart, on two prepared cookie sheets. With small metal spatula or back of spoon, spread batter into 2-inch rounds (see page 21). Bake until tops are shiny and cracked, about 13 minutes, rotating cookie sheets between upper and lower oven racks halfway through baking. Cool 10 minutes on cookie sheet. With wide metal spatula, transfer cookies to wire racks to cool completely.

5 Repeat with remaining batter.

EACH COOKIE: ABOUT 100 CALORIES | 1G PROTEIN | 9G CARBOHYDRATE | 7G TOTAL FAT (3G SATURATED) | 1G FIBER | 14MG CHOLESTEROL | 45MG SODIUM

RICH CHOCOLATE-CHERRY COOKIES

These luscious cookies will remind you why chocolate and cherries are a classic combination.

ACTIVE TIME: 30 MINUTES · **BAKE TIME:** 13 MINUTES PER BATCH
MAKES: 36 COOKIES

8   SQUARES (8 OUNCES) SEMISWEET CHOCOLATE, COARSELY CHOPPED

6   TABLESPOONS BUTTER OR MARGARINE, CUT INTO PIECES

¾   CUP SUGAR

2   TEASPOONS VANILLA EXTRACT

2   LARGE EGGS

¼   CUP ALL-PURPOSE FLOUR

¼   CUP UNSWEETENED COCOA

¼   TEASPOON BAKING POWDER

¼   TEASPOON SALT

1   PACKAGE (6 OUNCES) SEMISWEET CHOCOLATE CHIPS (1 CUP)

1   CUP DRIED TART CHERRIES

1 Preheat oven to 350°F. In 3-quart saucepan, melt chocolate and butter over low heat, stirring frequently. Remove saucepan from heat. With wire whisk, stir in sugar and vanilla until blended. Whisk in eggs, one at a time. With wooden spoon, stir in flour, cocoa, baking powder, and salt. Add chocolate chips and cherries; stir just until evenly mixed.

2 Drop dough by rounded tablespoons, 1½ inches apart, on ungreased large cookie sheet. Bake until tops of cookies are set, 13 to 15 minutes. Cool on cookie sheet on wire rack 1 minute. With wide metal spatula, transfer cookies to wire rack to cool completely.

3 Repeat with remaining dough.

EACH COOKIE: ABOUT 105 CALORIES | 1G PROTEIN | 16G CARBOHYDRATE | 5G TOTAL FAT (1G SATURATED) | 0.5G FIBER | 12MG CHOLESTEROL | 55MG SODIUM

TRIPLE-CHOCOLATE CHUBBIES

We added more chocolate, walnuts, and pecans to a dense brownie-like batter to create a big, fat cookie that became an instant hit in our test kitchen.

ACTIVE TIME: 25 MINUTES · **BAKE TIME:** 14 MINUTES PER BATCH

MAKES: 24 COOKIES

¼ CUP ALL-PURPOSE FLOUR

¼ CUP UNSWEETENED COCOA

½ TEASPOON BAKING POWDER

¼ TEASPOON SALT

8 SQUARES (8 OUNCES) SEMISWEET CHOCOLATE, CHOPPED

6 TABLESPOONS BUTTER OR MARGARINE, CUT INTO PIECES

1 CUP SUGAR

2 TEASPOONS VANILLA EXTRACT

2 LARGE EGGS

1 PACKAGE (6 OUNCES) SEMISWEET CHOCOLATE CHIPS (1 CUP)

½ CUP WALNUTS, CHOPPED

1 Preheat oven to 350°F. In small bowl, stir together flour, cocoa, baking powder, and salt.

2 In 3-quart saucepan, melt chopped chocolate and butter over low heat, stirring frequently, until smooth. Pour into large bowl; cool to lukewarm. Stir in sugar and vanilla until blended. Stir in eggs, one at a time, until well blended. Add flour mixture and stir until combined (batter will be thin). Stir in chocolate chips, pecans, and walnuts.

3 Drop batter by heaping tablespoons, 1½ inches apart, on ungreased large cookie sheet. Bake until set, 14 minutes. Cool on cookie sheet on wire rack 2 minutes. With wide metal spatula, carefully transfer cookies to wire rack to cool completely.

EACH COOKIE: ABOUT 180 CALORIES | 2G PROTEIN | 21G CARBOHYDRATE | 11G TOTAL FAT (5G SATURATED) | 1G FIBER | 26MG CHOLESTEROL | 70MG SODIUM

CHEWY PEANUT BUTTER COOKIES

These cookies work best with supermarket brands of peanut butter. The crosshatch pattern is traditional on peanut butter cookies, but you'll get no complaints if the tops are flattened with a spatula or spoon.

ACTIVE TIME: 35 MINUTES PLUS CHILLING · **BAKE TIME:** 12 MINUTES PER BATCH
MAKES: 60 COOKIES

2¾ CUPS ALL-PURPOSE FLOUR	1 CUP CREAMY PEANUT BUTTER
1 TEASPOON BAKING POWDER	1 CUP PACKED BROWN SUGAR
½ TEASPOON BAKING SODA	½ CUP GRANULATED SUGAR
¼ TEASPOON SALT	2 TABLESPOONS DARK CORN SYRUP
1 CUP BUTTER OR MARGARINE (2 STICKS), SOFTENED	2 TEASPOONS VANILLA EXTRACT
	2 LARGE EGGS

1 Preheat oven to 375°F. In medium bowl, combine flour, baking powder, baking soda, and salt.

2 In large bowl, with mixer at medium speed, beat butter, peanut butter, and brown and granulated sugars until creamy, occasionally scraping bowl with rubber spatula. Beat in corn syrup, vanilla, then eggs, one at a time, beating well after each addition. At low speed, gradually add flour mixture; beat just until blended, occasionally scraping bowl. Cover and refrigerate dough 30 minutes for easier shaping.

3 Shape dough by rounded tablespoons into 1½-inch balls. Place balls, 2 inches apart, on ungreased large cookie sheet. With floured tines of fork, press and flatten each ball, making a crisscross pattern (see Making Crosshatch Marks, opposite). Bake until pale golden, 12 to 13 minutes. With wide metal spatula, transfer cookies to wire rack to cool.

4 Repeat with remaining dough.

EACH COOKIE: ABOUT 100 CALORIES | 2G PROTEIN | 11G CARBOHYDRATE | 6G TOTAL FAT (3G SATURATED) | 1G FIBER | 16MG CHOLESTEROL | 85MG SODIUM

MAKING CROSSHATCH MARKS

Whether you drop the dough or shape it into balls, flattening the peanut butter dough with a fork gives it its classic finish. To avoid stickiness, first dip tines of fork in a little flour.

DROP SUGAR COOKIES

This simple old-time recipe is quick and delicious. To dress these cookies up for a party, sprinkle them with colored sugar before baking or drizzle them with melted chocolate after they come out of the oven.

ACTIVE TIME: 10 MINUTES · **BAKE TIME:** 10 MINUTES PER BATCH
MAKES: 42 COOKIES

1⅓ CUPS ALL-PURPOSE FLOUR

¾ TEASPOON BAKING POWDER

¼ TEASPOON SALT

½ CUP BUTTER OR MARGARINE
(1 STICK), SOFTENED

1 CUP SUGAR

1 LARGE EGG

1 TEASPOON VANILLA EXTRACT

1 Preheat oven to 350°F. In small bowl, combine flour, baking powder, and salt.

2 In large bowl, with mixer at medium speed, beat butter and sugar until light and fluffy. Beat in egg and vanilla until blended. Reduce speed to low; beat in flour mixture just until combined, scraping bowl with rubber spatula.

3 Drop dough by heaping teaspoons, 2 inches apart, on two ungreased cookie sheets. Bake until edges are browned, 10 to 12 minutes, rotating cookie sheets between upper and lower oven racks halfway through baking. With wide metal spatula, transfer cookies to wire racks to cool completely.

4 Repeat with remaining dough.

EACH COOKIE: ABOUT 55 CALORIES | 1G PROTEIN | 8G CARBOHYDRATE | 2G TOTAL FAT (1G SATURATED) | 0G FIBER | 11MG CHOLESTEROL | 46MG SODIUM

DROP BROWN-SUGAR COOKIES

These easy cookies are whipped up in a saucepan instead of a bowl. The combination of brown sugar and butter gives them the flavor and aroma of butterscotch.

ACTIVE TIME: 30 MINUTES · **BAKE TIME:** 10 MINUTES PER BATCH
MAKES: 72 COOKIES

1½ CUPS ALL-PURPOSE FLOUR

½ TEASPOON BAKING SODA

½ TEASPOON BAKING POWDER

¼ TEASPOON SALT

⅛ TEASPOON GROUND NUTMEG

¾ CUP BUTTER (1½ STICKS), CUT INTO PIECES

1 CUP PACKED LIGHT BROWN SUGAR

2 LARGE EGGS

1½ TEASPOONS VANILLA EXTRACT

1 Preheat oven to 350°F. Grease and flour two large cookie sheets. In small bowl, stir together flour, baking soda, baking powder, salt, and nutmeg.
2 In 3-quart saucepan, heat butter and brown sugar to boiling over low heat, stirring. Remove saucepan from heat. Stir in flour mixture, eggs, and vanilla until combined. Set saucepan in skillet of warm water.
3 Drop dough by rounded teaspoons, 1 inch apart, on two prepared cookie sheets. Bake until edges are browned and centers are set, 10 minutes, rotating sheets between upper and lower oven racks halfway through baking. Cool on cookie sheets on wire racks 1 minute. With wide metal spatula, transfer cookies to wire racks to cool completely.
4 Repeat with remaining cookie dough.

EACH COOKIE: ABOUT 50 CALORIES | 1G PROTEIN | 6G CARBOHYDRATE | 3G TOTAL FAT (2G SATURATED) | 0G FIBER | 13MG CHOLESTEROL | 50MG SODIUM

GRANDMA'S OATMEAL-RAISIN COOKIES

These family favorites bake up crisp and golden. If you prefer softer oatmeal cookies, reduce the baking time by about two minutes, and store them in a tight container with a slice of fresh bread or apple. Replace the bread or apple every other day.

ACTIVE TIME: 15 MINUTES · **BAKE TIME:** 15 MINUTES PER BATCH
MAKES: 24 COOKIES

¾ CUP ALL-PURPOSE FLOUR

½ TEASPOON BAKING SODA

¼ TEASPOON SALT

½ CUP BUTTER OR MARGARINE (1 STICK), SOFTENED

½ CUP GRANULATED SUGAR

⅓ CUP PACKED LIGHT BROWN SUGAR

1 LARGE EGG

2 TEASPOONS VANILLA EXTRACT

1½ CUPS OLD-FASHIONED OR QUICK-COOKING OATS, UNCOOKED

¾ CUP DARK SEEDLESS RAISINS OR CHOPPED PITTED PRUNES

1 Preheat oven to 350°F. In small bowl, combine flour, baking soda, and salt.

2 In large bowl, with mixer at medium speed, beat butter and granulated and brown sugars until light and fluffy. Beat in egg and vanilla until blended. Reduce speed to low; beat in flour mixture just until blended. With wooden spoon, stir in oats and raisins.

3 Drop dough by heaping tablespoons, 2 inches apart, on two ungreased large cookie sheets. Bake until golden, about 15 minutes, rotating cookie sheets between upper and lower oven racks halfway through baking. With wide metal spatula, transfer cookies to wire racks to cool completely.

4 Repeat with remaining dough.

EACH COOKIE: ABOUT 115 CALORIES | 2G PROTEIN | 17G CARBOHYDRATE | 4G TOTAL FAT (2G SATURATED) | 1G FIBER | 19MG CHOLESTEROL | 94MG SODIUM

MCINTOSH OATMEAL COOKIES

Chock-full of apples, raisins, and walnuts, these big cookies bake up rich, dense, and moist, with a hint of cinnamon.

ACTIVE TIME: 30 MINUTES · **BAKE TIME:** 20 MINUTES PER BATCH
MAKES: 24 COOKIES

1   CUP MARGARINE OR BUTTER (2 STICKS), SOFTENED

1½ CUPS SUGAR

1½ CUPS ALL-PURPOSE FLOUR

1   TEASPOON BAKING SODA

1   TEASPOON GROUND CINNAMON

½   TEASPOON SALT

1   TEASPOON VANILLA EXTRACT

2   LARGE EGGS

2   MEDIUM-SIZE MCINTOSH APPLES, PEELED, CORED, AND DICED (ABOUT 2 CUPS)

3   CUPS QUICK-COOKING OATS, UNCOOKED

1   CUP DARK SEEDLESS RAISINS

¾   CUP WALNUTS, CHOPPED

1 Preheat oven to 350°F.

2 In large bowl, with mixer at medium speed, beat margarine and sugar until light and fluffy, about 5 minutes. Add flour, baking soda, cinnamon, salt, vanilla, and eggs; beat just until blended, occasionally scraping bowl with rubber spatula. With wooden spoon, stir in apples, oats, raisins, and walnuts.

3 Drop dough by level ¼ cups, about 3 inches apart, on two ungreased large cookie sheets. Bake until golden, 20 to 25 minutes, rotating cookie sheets between upper and lower oven racks halfway through baking time. With wide metal spatula, transfer cookies to wire racks to cool completely.

4 Repeat with remaining dough.

EACH COOKIE: ABOUT 275 CALORIES | 5G PROTEIN | 39G CARBOHYDRATE | 12G TOTAL FAT (2G SATURATED) | 1G FIBER | 18MG CHOLESTEROL | 205MG SODIUM

CHOCOLATE-CHERRY OATMEAL COOKIES

For an all grown-up version of home-baked oatmeal cookies, we swap in dried cherries and semisweet chocolate chips for the raisins. For chewy cookies, bake the minimum time; for crispy, bake a few minutes longer.

ACTIVE TIME: 45 MINUTES PLUS COOLING · **BAKE TIME:** 12 MINUTES PER BATCH

MAKES: 54 COOKIES

---

3   CUPS ALL-PURPOSE FLOUR

4   TEASPOONS BAKING SODA

1   TEASPOON SALT

1½ CUPS GRANULATED SUGAR

1½ CUPS PACKED BROWN SUGAR

1½ CUPS BUTTER OR MARGARINE
    (3 STICKS), SOFTENED

4   LARGE EGGS

4   TEASPOONS VANILLA EXTRACT

6   CUPS OLD-FASHIONED OATS,
    UNCOOKED

2   CUPS DRIED TART CHERRIES OR
    RAISINS

2   PACKAGES (6 OUNCES EACH)
    SEMISWEET CHOCOLATE CHIPS
    (2 CUPS)

---

1 Preheat oven to 350°F. Grease two large cookie sheets. In small bowl, with wire whisk, stir flour, baking soda, and salt until blended.

2 In large bowl, with mixer at medium speed, beat granulated and brown sugars and butter until creamy, occasionally scraping bowl with rubber spatula. Beat in eggs, one at a time, beating well after each addition. Beat in vanilla. Reduce speed to low; gradually beat in flour mixture just until blended, occasionally scraping bowl.

3 With wooden spoon, stir in oats, dried cherries, and chocolate chips until well combined.

4 Drop dough by rounded measuring tablespoons, 2 inches apart, onto two prepared cookie sheets. Bake cookies until tops are golden, 12 to 14 minutes, rotating cookie sheets between upper and lower racks halfway through baking. With wide spatula, transfer cookies to wire racks to cool.

5 Repeat with remaining dough.

EACH COOKIE: ABOUT 100 CALORIES | 1G PROTEIN | 15G CARBOHYDRATE | 4G TOTAL FAT (2G SATURATED) | 1G FIBER | 15MG CHOLESTEROL | 100MG SODIUM

LOW-FAT OATMEAL-RAISIN COOKIES

With their mellow brown sugar and moist raisins, these cookies taste so good no one will ever know they're low-fat. We did it by using light corn-oil spread and egg whites.

ACTIVE TIME: 15 MINUTES · **BAKE TIME:** 10 MINUTES PER BATCH
MAKES: 48 COOKIES

2	CUPS ALL-PURPOSE FLOUR	2	LARGE EGG WHITES
1	TEASPOON BAKING SODA	1	LARGE EGG
½	TEASPOON SALT	2	TEASPOONS VANILLA EXTRACT
½	CUP LIGHT CORN-OIL SPREAD (1 STICK), 56% TO 60% FAT	1	CUP QUICK-COOKING OATS, UNCOOKED
¾	CUP PACKED DARK BROWN SUGAR	½	CUP DARK SEEDLESS RAISINS
½	CUP GRANULATED SUGAR		

1 Preheat oven to 375°F. Grease two large cookie sheets. In medium bowl, combine flour, baking soda, and salt.

2 In large bowl, with mixer at low speed, beat corn-oil spread and brown and granulated sugars until well combined. Increase speed to high; beat until mixture is light and fluffy. Add egg whites, whole egg, and vanilla; beat until blended. With wooden spoon, stir in flour mixture, oats, and raisins until combined.

3 Drop dough by level tablespoons, 2 inches apart, on two prepared cookie sheets. Bake until golden, 10 to 12 minutes, rotating cookie sheets between upper and lower oven racks halfway through baking. With wide metal spatula, transfer cookies to wire racks to cool completely.

4 Repeat with remaining dough.

EACH COOKIE: ABOUT 65 CALORIES | 1G PROTEIN | 12G CARBOHYDRATE | 2G TOTAL FAT (0G SATURATED) | 1G FIBER | 4MG CHOLESTEROL | 72MG SODIUM

MORAVIAN SPICE CRISPS

Our paper-thin spice crisps are a less labor-intensive version of the originals, which were brought by Moravian settlers to Winston-Salem, North Carolina, in the 1700s.

ACTIVE TIME: 30 MINUTES · **BAKE TIME:** 8 MINUTES PER BATCH
MAKES: 36 COOKIES

¾ CUP ALL-PURPOSE FLOUR

½ TEASPOON BAKING POWDER

½ TEASPOON GROUND CINNAMON

½ TEASPOON GROUND GINGER

½ TEASPOON GROUND WHITE PEPPER

¼ TEASPOON GROUND CLOVES

¼ TEASPOON BAKING SODA

¼ TEASPOON SALT

⅓ CUP PACKED LIGHT BROWN SUGAR

3 TABLESPOONS MARGARINE OR BUTTER, SOFTENED

¼ CUP LIGHT (MILD) MOLASSES

1 Preheat oven to 350°F. Grease large cookie sheet.

2 In large bowl, combine flour, baking powder, cinnamon, ginger, white pepper, cloves, baking soda, and salt.

3 In another large bowl, with mixer at low speed, beat brown sugar and margarine until blended. Increase speed to high; beat until creamy, about 2 minutes. At medium speed, beat in molasses until blended. With wooden spoon, stir in flour mixture.

4 Drop dough by rounded teaspoons, about 4 inches apart, on prepared cookie sheet. With finger, press each into a 2-inch round. Bake until cookies spread and darken, 8 to 10 minutes. Cool on cookie sheet on wire rack 3 minutes. With wide metal spatula, transfer cookies to wire rack to cool completely.

5 Repeat with remaining dough. Store cookies in tightly covered container.

EACH COOKIE: ABOUT 30 CALORIES | 0G PROTEIN | 6G CARBOHYDRATE | 1G TOTAL FAT (0G SATURATED) | 0G FIBER | 0MG CHOLESTEROL | 45MG SODIUM

SOFT APPLESAUCE-RAISIN COOKIES

A Granny Smith apple adds moisture and texture, while the lemon glaze gives an appealing shine to these old-fashioned beauties.

ACTIVE TIME: 35 MINUTES · **BAKE TIME:** 20 MINUTES
MAKES: 45 COOKIES

APPLESAUCE-RAISIN COOKIES

2   CUPS ALL-PURPOSE FLOUR

½   TEASPOON BAKING POWDER

½   TEASPOON BAKING SODA

½   TEASPOON GROUND CINNAMON

¼   TEASPOON GROUND ALLSPICE

¼   TEASPOON SALT

½   CUP BUTTER OR MARGARINE (1 STICK), SOFTENED

½   CUP GRANULATED SUGAR

¼   CUP PACKED BROWN SUGAR

1   LARGE EGG

1   CUP UNSWEETENED APPLESAUCE

1   TEASPOON VANILLA EXTRACT

1   MEDIUM GRANNY SMITH APPLE, PEELED, CORED, AND DICED

1   CUP DARK RAISINS

1   CUP WALNUTS (4 OUNCES), COARSELY CHOPPED (OPTIONAL)

LEMON GLAZE

1   CUP CONFECTIONERS' SUGAR

2   TABLESPOONS FRESH LEMON JUICE

1 Preheat oven to 375°F. Grease two large cookie sheets.

2 Prepare cookies: In medium bowl, combine flour, baking powder, baking soda, cinnamon, allspice, and salt.

3 In large bowl, with mixer at medium speed, beat butter and granulated and brown sugars until light and fluffy. Reduce speed to low; beat in egg, applesauce, and vanilla until well combined. Beat in flour mixture until blended. With wooden spoon, stir in apple, raisins, and walnuts, if using.

4 Drop dough by rounded tablespoons, 1 inch apart, on two prepared cookie sheets. Bake until lightly browned around edges and set, 20 to 22 minutes, rotating cookie sheets between upper and lower oven racks halfway through baking.

5 While cookies bake, prepare glaze: In small bowl, stir confectioners' sugar and lemon juice until smooth.

6 With wide metal spatula, transfer cookies to wire racks. With pastry brush, brush glaze over warm cookies; cool completely.

EACH COOKIE: ABOUT 80 CALORIES | 1G PROTEIN | 14G CARBOHYDRATE | 2G TOTAL FAT (1G SATURATED) | 0.5G FIBER | 11MG CHOLESTEROL | 55MG SODIUM

CHEWY MOLASSES-SPICE COOKIES

Dark, chewy, and warm with spices, these luscious cookies originated in Europe. Centuries ago spice cookies were made with black pepper and even mustard, just as these are.

ACTIVE TIME: 15 MINUTES · **BAKE TIME:** 13 MINUTES PER BATCH
MAKES: 42 COOKIES

2	CUPS ALL-PURPOSE FLOUR	⅛	TEASPOON GROUND MUSTARD
1½	TEASPOONS BAKING SODA	½	CUP BUTTER OR MARGARINE (1 STICK), SOFTENED
1	TEASPOON GROUND GINGER	¾	CUP PACKED DARK BROWN SUGAR
½	TEASPOON GROUND CINNAMON	½	CUP LIGHT (MILD) MOLASSES
¼	TEASPOON SALT	1	LARGE EGG
¼	TEASPOON FINELY GROUND BLACK PEPPER	1	TEASPOON VANILLA EXTRACT
⅛	TEASPOON GROUND CLOVES		

1 Preheat oven to 350°F. In small bowl, stir together flour, baking soda, ginger, cinnamon, salt, pepper, cloves, and mustard.

2 In large bowl, with mixer at medium speed, beat butter and brown sugar until smooth. Beat in molasses until combined. Reduce speed to low; beat in egg and vanilla until blended. Beat in flour mixture until combined, scraping bowl occasionally with rubber spatula.

3 Drop dough by rounded tablespoons, 3 inches apart, on ungreased large cookie sheet. Bake until flattened and evenly browned, 13 to 15 minutes. Cool on cookie sheet on wire rack 2 minutes. With wide metal spatula, transfer cookies to wire rack to cool completely.

4 Repeat with remaining cookie dough.

EACH COOKIE: ABOUT 70 CALORIES | 1G PROTEIN | 11G CARBOHYDRATE | 2G TOTAL FAT (1G SATURATED) | 0G FIBER | 11MG CHOLESTEROL | 85MG SODIUM

SOUR-CREAM COOKIES

Subtle nutmeg flavor and a light cakelike texture make these an elegant partner for a cup of afternoon tea.

ACTIVE TIME: 25 MINUTES **BAKE TIME:** 10 MINUTES PER BATCH

MAKES: 30 COOKIES

1¾ CUPS ALL-PURPOSE FLOUR

1 TEASPOON BAKING POWDER

½ TEASPOON SALT

¼ TEASPOON BAKING SODA

¼ TEASPOON GROUND NUTMEG

½ CUP BUTTER OR MARGARINE (1 STICK), SOFTENED

1 CUP PLUS 2 TABLESPOONS GRANULATED SUGAR

1 LARGE EGG

2 TEASPOONS VANILLA EXTRACT

½ CUP SOUR CREAM

1 Preheat oven to 400°F. Grease large cookie sheet.

2 In medium bowl, combine flour, baking powder, salt, baking soda, and nutmeg.

3 In large bowl, with mixer at medium speed, beat butter and 1 cup sugar until creamy, occasionally scraping bowl with rubber spatula. Beat in egg and vanilla, then sour cream, until well combined. With mixer at low speed, beat in flour mixture just until blended, occasionally scraping bowl.

4 Drop dough by rounded tablespoons, 2 inches apart, on prepared cookie sheet. Sprinkle lightly with some of remaining sugar. Bake until edges are lightly browned, 10 to 12 minutes. With wide metal spatula, transfer cookies to wire rack to cool.

5 Repeat with remaining dough and sugar.

EACH COOKIE: ABOUT 70 CALORIES | 1G PROTEIN | 11G CARBOHYDRATE | 2G TOTAL FAT (1G SATURATED) | 0G FIBER | 11MG CHOLESTEROL | 85MG SODIUM

LEMONY SOUR-CREAM COOKIES

A hint of lemon adds fresh, bright flavor to sour-cream cookies. For a sparkling finishing touch, buzz some granulated sugar and a piece of lemon rind in the food processor and sprinkle it over the tops.

PREP: 15 MINUTES · **BAKE:** 10 MINUTES PER BATCH
MAKES: 36 COOKIES

1	CUP ALL-PURPOSE FLOUR	½	CUP SUGAR
¼	TEASPOON BAKING SODA	½	CUP SOUR CREAM
¼	TEASPOON SALT	1	TEASPOON FRESHLY GRATED LEMON PEEL
6	TABLESPOONS BUTTER OR MARGARINE, SOFTENED	½	TEASPOON VANILLA EXTRACT

1 Preheat oven to 350°F. Grease two large cookie sheets. In small bowl, combine flour, baking soda, and salt.

2 In large bowl, with mixer at medium speed, beat butter until creamy. Gradually add sugar and beat until light and fluffy. Beat in sour cream, lemon peel, and vanilla. Reduce speed to low; beat in flour mixture just until blended.

3 Drop dough by rounded teaspoons, 1 inch apart, on two prepared cookie sheets. Bake until cookies are set and edges are golden, 10 to 12 minutes, rotating cookie sheets between upper and lower oven racks halfway through baking. Cool on cookie sheets on wire rack 1 minute. With wide metal spatula, transfer cookies to wire racks to cool completely.

4 Repeat with remaining dough.

EACH COOKIE: ABOUT 50 CALORIES | 0G PROTEIN | 6G CARBOHYDRATE | 3G TOTAL FAT (2G SATURATED) | 0G FIBER | 7MG CHOLESTEROL | 46MG SODIUM

COCONUT COOKIES

To make an attractive crisscross design on these coconut-packed drop cookies, simply flatten them with a fork. If the fork starts to get sticky, just dip the tines in a little flour. For photo of technique, see page 27.

ACTIVE TIME: 20 MINUTES · **BAKE TIME:** 15 MINUTES PER BATCH
MAKES: 72 COOKIES

2¾ CUPS ALL-PURPOSE FLOUR

1   TEASPOON BAKING POWDER

½   TEASPOON SALT

1   CUP BUTTER OR MARGARINE
    (2 STICKS), SOFTENED

1   CUP SUGAR

1   LARGE EGG

2   TABLESPOONS MILK

1   TEASPOON VANILLA EXTRACT

1½ CUPS FLAKED SWEETENED COCONUT

1 Preheat oven to 325°F. In medium bowl, combine flour, baking powder, and salt.

2 In large bowl, with mixer at medium speed, beat butter and sugar until light and fluffy. Beat in egg, milk, and vanilla. Reduce speed to low; beat in flour mixture just until blended. With wooden spoon, stir in coconut (dough will be crumbly). With hands, press dough together.

3 Drop dough by rounded teaspoons, 2 inches apart, on two ungreased cookie sheets. With fork, make crosshatch pattern in each cookie, flattening to ¼-inch thickness. Bake until edges are lightly browned, 15 to 17 minutes, rotating cookie sheets between upper and lower oven racks halfway through baking. With wide metal spatula, transfer cookies to wire racks to cool completely.

4 Repeat with remaining dough.

EACH COOKIE: ABOUT 45 CALORIES | 0G PROTEIN | 5G CARBOHYDRATE | 2G TOTAL FAT (2G SATURATED) | 0.5G FIBER | 7MG CHOLESTEROL | 41MG SODIUM

ALMOND MACAROONS

We added sliced almonds to these old-fashioned favorites to make them doubly delicious. Thanks to prepared almond paste, you can whip them up in half the time it took Grandma.

ACTIVE TIME: 20 MINUTES · **BAKE TIME:** 18 MINUTES PER BATCH
MAKES: 30 COOKIES

1   TUBE OR CAN (7 TO 8 OUNCES) ALMOND PASTE, CUT INTO 1-INCH PIECES

⅓   CUP CONFECTIONERS' SUGAR

1   LARGE EGG WHITE

½   CUP SLICED NATURAL ALMONDS

1   Preheat oven to 325°F. Evenly grease and flour large cookie sheet.

2   In small bowl, with mixer at low speed, beat almond paste until crumbly. Add confectioners' sugar and egg white; beat until well blended (dough will be wet and sticky).

3   Place almonds on waxed paper. With lightly floured hands, roll dough into 1-inch balls. Roll balls in almonds, gently pressing to coat. Place balls, 1 inch apart, on prepared cookie sheet.

4   Bake until golden, 18 to 20 minutes. With wide metal spatula, transfer cookies to wire racks to cool completely.

EACH COOKIE: ABOUT 50 CALORIES | 1G PROTEIN | 5G CARBOHYDRATE | 3G TOTAL FAT (0G SATURATED) | 0G FIBER | 0MG CHOLESTEROL | 3MG SODIUM

CHOCOLATE-HAZELNUT MACAROONS

Chocolate and hazelnut is a delectable flavor combination. Although these chewy-crisp cookies are delicious on their own, you can make them even more elegant by sandwiching two together with some melted chocolate.

ACTIVE TIME: 30 MINUTES · **BAKE TIME:** 10 MINUTES PER BATCH

MAKES: 30 COOKIES

1   CUP HAZELNUTS (FILBERTS, 5 OUNCES)

1   CUP SUGAR

¼   CUP UNSWEETENED COCOA

1   SQUARE (1 OUNCE) UNSWEETENED CHOCOLATE, CHOPPED

⅛   TEASPOON SALT

2   LARGE EGG WHITES

1   TEASPOON VANILLA EXTRACT

1 Preheat oven to 350°F. Toast and skin hazelnuts (see page 75). Line two large cookie sheets with foil.

2 In food processor with knife blade attached, process hazelnuts, sugar, cocoa, chocolate, and salt until nuts and chocolate are finely ground. Add egg whites and vanilla and process until blended.

3 Drop dough by rounded teaspoons, using another spoon to release batter, 2 inches apart, on prepared cookie sheets. Bake until tops feel firm when pressed lightly, 10 minutes, rotating sheets between upper and lower racks halfway through baking. Cool on cookie sheets on wire racks.

4 Repeat with remaining cookie dough.

EACH COOKIE: ABOUT 60 CALORIES | 1G PROTEIN | 8G CARBOHYDRATE | 3G TOTAL FAT (1G SATURATED) | 0.5G FIBER | 0MG CHOLESTEROL | 15MG SODIUM

ALMOND TUILES

These crisp, curved cookies—molded over a rolling pin while still hot—were named for the terra-cotta roof tiles used in the south of France. If you want to save time, you can cool them on a flat surface as you would other drop cookies—they'll taste just as delicious.

ACTIVE TIME: 30 MINUTES · **BAKE TIME:** 5 MINUTES PER BATCH
MAKES: 30 COOKIES

3   LARGE EGG WHITES

¾   CUP CONFECTIONERS' SUGAR

½   CUP ALL-PURPOSE FLOUR

6   TABLESPOONS BUTTER, MELTED
    (DO NOT USE MARGARINE)

¼   TEASPOON SALT

¼   TEASPOON ALMOND EXTRACT

⅔   CUP SLICED ALMONDS

1 Preheat oven to 350°F. Grease large cookie sheet.

2 In large bowl, with wire whisk, beat egg whites, confectioners' sugar, and flour until blended and smooth. Beat in melted butter, salt, and almond extract until blended.

3 Drop 1 heaping teaspoon batter on prepared cookie sheet. With back of spoon, spread in circular motion to make 3-inch round (see Step 1 photo, opposite). Repeat to make 4 cookies in all, placing them 3 inches apart. (Do not place more than 4 cookies on sheet.) Sprinkle with some almonds (do not overlap).

4 Bake until golden around edges, 5 to 7 minutes. With wide metal spatula, quickly lift cookies, one at a time, and drape over rolling pin or other cylinder to curve cookies (see Step 2 photo, opposite). When firm, transfer to wire racks to cool completely. (If you like, omit shaping and cool cookies flat.) If cookies become too firm to shape, briefly return to oven to soften.

5 Repeat with remaining batter and almonds. (Batter will become slightly thicker upon standing.)

EACH COOKIE: ABOUT 55 CALORIES | 1G PROTEIN | 5G CARBOHYDRATE | 4G TOTAL FAT (2G SATURATED) | 0G FIBER | 6MG CHOLESTEROL | 48MG SODIUM

SHAPING ALMOND TUILES

Step 1: Drop the Almond Tuile batter on a greased cookie sheet and spread it in a circular motion with the back of a spoon.

Step 2: After baking, transfer hot cookies to a rolling pin or other cylindrical object and allow to cool in the curved shape.

BRANDY SNAPS

The alcohol disappears in the oven, leaving only the mellow flavor of the brandy behind, so no need to worry about giving the kids a taste. You can make the cookies flat or spiral them around the handle of a wooden spoon. For photos of these techniques, see page 45.

ACTIVE TIME: 25 MINUTES · **BAKE TIME:** 5 MINUTES PER BATCH

MAKES: 24 COOKIES

½ CUP BUTTER (1 STICK, DO NOT USE MARGARINE)

3 TABLESPOONS LIGHT (MILD) MOLASSES

½ CUP ALL-PURPOSE FLOUR

½ CUP SUGAR

1 TEASPOON GROUND GINGER

¼ TEASPOON SALT

2 TABLESPOONS BRANDY

1 Preheat oven to 350°F. Grease large cookie sheet.

2 In 2-quart saucepan, melt butter and molasses over medium-low heat, stirring occasionally, until smooth. Remove from heat. With wooden spoon, stir in flour, sugar, ginger, and salt until blended and smooth; stir in brandy. Set saucepan in skillet of hot water to keep warm.

3 Drop 1 teaspoon batter on prepared cookie sheet; with small metal spatula or back of spoon, spread in circular motion to make 4-inch round (during baking, batter will spread and fill in any thin areas). Repeat to make 4 rounds in all, placing them 2 inches apart. (Do not place more than 4 cookies on sheet.)

4 Bake until golden brown, about 5 minutes. Cool on cookie sheet on wire rack just until edges have set, 30 to 60 seconds. Then, with wide metal spatula, quickly flip cookies over.

5 Working as quickly as possible, roll up each cookie around handle of wooden spoon or dowel about ½ inch in diameter. If cookies become too hard to roll, briefly return to oven to soften. As each cookie is shaped, slip off spoon handle and cool completely on wire rack.

6 Repeat with remaining batter.

EACH COOKIE: ABOUT 70 CALORIES | 0G PROTEIN | 8G CARBOHYDRATE | 4G TOTAL FAT (2G SATURATED) | 0G FIBER | 10MG CHOLESTEROL | 64MG SODIUM

BLACK-AND-WHITE COOKIES

These giant sugar cookies decorated with half chocolate and half vanilla frosting are popular in New York City bakeries. You can also enjoy them the way they do across the Hudson in New Jersey by just eliminating the frosting.

ACTIVE TIME: 20 MINUTES PLUS COOLING · **BAKE TIME:** 15 MINUTES
MAKES: 12 COOKIES

---

2 CUPS ALL-PURPOSE FLOUR	2 TEASPOONS VANILLA EXTRACT
½ TEASPOON BAKING SODA	½ CUP BUTTERMILK
¼ TEASPOON SALT	1¾ CUPS CONFECTIONERS' SUGAR
10 TABLESPOONS BUTTER OR MARGARINE (1¼ STICKS), SOFTENED	2 TABLESPOONS LIGHT CORN SYRUP
1 CUP GRANULATED SUGAR	8 TO 10 TEASPOONS WATER, WARMED
2 LARGE EGGS	¼ CUP UNSWEETENED COCOA

1 Preheat oven to 350°F. In small bowl, stir together flour, baking soda, and salt.

2 In large bowl, with mixer at medium speed, beat butter and granulated sugar until creamy. Beat in eggs and vanilla until blended. Reduce speed to low; add flour mixture alternately with buttermilk, beginning and ending with flour mixture. Beat just until combined, scraping bowl occasionally with rubber spatula.

3 Drop dough by ¼ cups, about 3 inches apart, on two ungreased large cookie sheets. Bake until edges begin to brown and tops spring back when lightly touched with finger, 15 to 17 minutes, rotating sheets between upper and lower racks halfway through baking. With wide metal spatula, transfer cookies to wire racks to cool completely.

4. When cookies are cool, prepare white glaze: In medium bowl, mix 1¼ cups confectioners' sugar, 1 tablespoon corn syrup, and 5 to 6 teaspoons water, 1 teaspoon at a time, to good spreading consistency. Turn cookies over, flat side up. With small metal spatula, spread glaze over half of each cookie. Allow glaze to set 20 minutes.

5 Meanwhile, prepare chocolate glaze: In small bowl, stir together remaining ½ cup confectioners' sugar, cocoa, remaining 1 tablespoon corn syrup, and remaining 3 to 4 teaspoons water, 1 teaspoon at a time, to spreading consistency. With clean small metal spatula, spread chocolate glaze over unglazed half of each cookie. Let glaze set completely, at least 1 hour.

EACH COOKIE: ABOUT 280 CALORIES | 3G PROTEIN | 46G CARBOHYDRATE | 9G TOTAL FAT
(6G SATURATED) | 1G FIBER | 53MG CHOLESTEROL | 190MG SODIUM

LOLLIPOP COOKIES

You can entertain children for quite a while by letting them decorate these fun sweets with a variety of candies. Jelly beans, gumdrops, and chocolate pieces are just some of the options.

ACTIVE TIME: 45 MINUTES · **BAKE TIME:** 18 MINUTES PER BATCH
MAKES: 12 COOKIES

1   PACKAGE (18¼ OUNCES) FAVORITE CAKE MIX

½   CUP BUTTER OR MARGARINE (1 STICK), MELTED

2   LARGE EGGS

12 WOODEN ICE CREAM BAR STICKS

VANILLA FROSTING (SEE BELOW) OR 1 CAN (16 OUNCES) VANILLA FROSTING

FOOD COLORING

COLORED DÉCORS; ASSORTED CANDIES SUCH AS JELLY BEANS, GUMDROPS, CANDY-COATED CHOCOLATE PIECES, NONPAREILS, BLACK AND/OR RED SHOESTRING LICORICE

1   Preheat oven to 350°F. Grease large cookie sheet.
2   In medium bowl, with wooden spoon, stir cake mix, melted butter, and eggs until dough is blended and smooth. Drop dough by scant ¼ cups, about 5 inches apart, onto cookie sheet to make 4 cookies (dough will be sticky). Place one end of an ice cream bar stick into each mound of dough. With hand, flatten each into a 2½-inch round.
3   Bake cookies until lightly browned around edges, 18 to 20 minutes. With wide metal spatula, transfer cookies to wire racks to cool. Repeat twice with remaining dough.
4   To decorate cookies, tint frosting with food colorings as desired. Spread about 2 tablespoons frosting on each cookie. Top frosting with décors and candies.

VANILLA FROSTING

In large bowl, with mixer at low speed, beat **2¼ cups confectioners' sugar**, **6 tablespoons butter**, softened, **3 tablespoons whole milk**, and **1½ teaspoons vanilla extract** until blended. Increase speed to medium-high; beat until light and fluffy, occasionally scraping bowl with rubber spatula. Makes about 1½ cups.

EACH FROSTED COOKIE: ABOUT 430 CALORIES | 3G PROTEIN | 61G CARBOHYDRATE | 20G TOTAL FAT (8G SATURATED) | 1G FIBER | 58MG CHOLESTEROL | 420MG SODIUM

WHOOPIE PIES

We discovered these soft, marshmallow-filled chocolate sandwiches at a farmers' market and just loved them. So we re-created the recipe and now you can bake them at home.

ACTIVE TIME: 30 MINUTES PLUS COOLING · **BAKE TIME:** 12 MINUTES
MAKES: 12 WHOOPIE PIES

COOKIES

2   CUPS ALL-PURPOSE FLOUR

1   CUP GRANULATED SUGAR

½   CUP UNSWEETENED COCOA

1   TEASPOON BAKING SODA

6   TABLESPOONS BUTTER OR MARGARINE, MELTED

¾   CUP MILK

1   LARGE EGG

1   TEASPOON VANILLA EXTRACT

¼   TEASPOON SALT

MARSHMALLOW-CREME FILLING

6   TABLESPOONS BUTTER OR MARGARINE, SLIGHTLY SOFTENED

1   CUP CONFECTIONERS' SUGAR

1   JAR (7 TO 7½ OUNCES) MARSHMALLOW CREME

1   TEASPOON VANILLA EXTRACT

1   Preheat oven to 350°F. Grease two large cookie sheets.

2   Prepare cookies: In large bowl, combine flour, granulated sugar, cocoa, and baking soda. Stir in melted butter, milk, egg, vanilla, and salt until smooth.

3   Drop dough by heaping tablespoons, 2 inches apart, on prepared cookie sheets. (There will be 12 rounds per sheet.) Bake until cookies are puffy and toothpick inserted in center comes out clean, 12 to 14 minutes, rotating sheets between upper and lower racks halfway through baking. With wide metal spatula, transfer cookies to wire racks to cool completely.

4   When cookies are cool, prepare filling: In large bowl, with mixer at medium speed, beat softened butter until smooth. Reduce speed to low; gradually beat in confectioners' sugar. Beat in marshmallow creme and vanilla until smooth.

5   Spread 1 rounded tablespoon filling on flat side of 12 cookies. Top with remaining cookies.

EACH WHOOPIE PIE: ABOUT 365 CALORIES | 4G PROTEIN | 59G CARBOHYDRATE | 14G TOTAL FAT (8G SATURATED) | 1.5G FIBER | 51MG CHOLESTEROL | 290MG SODIUM

ROLLED & CUT-OUT COOKIES

Rolled cookies are a gift of love, works of art to be appreciated visually before savoring. However that doesn't mean they are just for special occasions. Most rolled-cookie doughs are very easy to make, a perfect rainy-weekend activity to enjoy with your family.

They are great make-aheads, too. You can prepare several batches at once and keep the dough in the freezer for up to three months, all ready to roll out and bake.

Here are some tips that will make it easy.

- **Chill the dough before rolling.** A few rolled-cookie doughs are stiff enough to roll out shortly after they are prepared, but most require several hours of chilling. For convenience, you might want to make the dough a day ahead and refrigerate it overnight.
- **For easier rolling,** dust the work surface lightly and evenly with flour before you roll out the dough. Also rub the rolling pin with flour to keep it from sticking.
- **For easier cleanup,** you can roll out dough between sheets of waxed paper. Flour both the waxed paper and your rolling pin.
- **Roll out one portion of chilled dough at a time** and keep the remaining dough well wrapped in the refrigerator. It's difficult to roll warm, sticky dough.
- **If chilled dough cracks when rolled,** let it stand at room temperature to soften slightly, then try again.
- **Cut out cookies as close together as possible** so that you have less dough to reroll.

Best Linzer Cookies (page 56)

BEST LINZER COOKIES

A half pound of pecans goes into these raspberry jam–filled tartlike treats. For photo, see page 54.

ACTIVE TIME: 1 HOUR PLUS CHILLING AND COOLING · **BAKE TIME:** 17 MINUTES PER BATCH
MAKES: 48 COOKIES

1 (8-OUNCE) BAG PECANS	2 TEASPOONS VANILLA EXTRACT
½ CUP CORNSTARCH	¾ TEASPOON SALT
1½ CUPS (3 STICKS) BUTTER, SOFTENED (DO NOT USE MARGARINE)	1 LARGE EGG
	2¾ CUPS ALL-PURPOSE FLOUR
1⅓ CUPS CONFECTIONERS' SUGAR	¾ CUP SEEDLESS RED RASPBERRY JAM

1 In food processor with knife blade attached, pulse pecans and cornstarch until pecans are finely ground.

2 In large bowl, with mixer on low speed, beat butter and 1 cup confectioners' sugar until mixed. Increase speed to high; beat 2 minutes or until light and fluffy, occasionally scraping bowl with rubber spatula. At medium speed, beat in vanilla, salt, and egg. Reduce speed to low; gradually beat in flour and pecan mixture just until blended, occasionally scraping bowl.

3 Divide dough into 4 equal pieces; flatten each into a disk. Wrap each disk with plastic wrap and refrigerate 4 to 5 hours or until dough is firm enough to roll.

4 Preheat oven to 325°F. Remove 1 disk of dough from refrigerator; if necessary, let stand 10 to 15 minutes at room temperature for easier rolling. On lightly floured surface, with floured rolling pin, roll dough ⅛ inch thick. With floured 2¼-inch fluted round, plain round, or holiday-shaped cookie cutter, cut dough into as many cookies as possible. With floured 1- to 1¼-inch fluted round, plain round, or holiday-shaped cookie cutter, cut out centers from half of cookies. Wrap and refrigerate trimmings. With lightly floured spatula, carefully place cookies, 1 inch apart, on ungreased large cookie sheet.

5 Bake cookies 17 to 20 minutes or until edges are lightly browned. Transfer cookies to wire rack to cool. Repeat with remaining dough and trimmings.

6 When cookies are cool, sprinkle remaining ⅓ cup confectioners' sugar through sieve over cookies with cut-out centers.

7 In small bowl, stir jam with fork until smooth. Spread scant measuring teaspoon jam on top of whole cookies; place cut-out cookies on top.

EACH COOKIE: ABOUT 115 CALORIES | 16G PROTEIN | 11G CARBOHYDRATE | 8G TOTAL FAT (3G SATURATED) | 1G FIBER | 17MG CHOLESTEROL | 80MG SODIUM

WHOLE-WHEAT SUGAR COOKIES

Using white whole-wheat flour adds healthy whole-grain goodness to this low-fat variation on the classic (pages 58–59). If you like, dress them up using our decorating tips on pages 14–15.

ACTIVE TIME: 1 HOUR PLUS CHILLING AND COOLING · **BAKE TIME:** 10 MINUTES PER BATCH
MAKES: 72 COOKIES

1 CUP ALL-PURPOSE FLOUR	½ CUP TRANS FAT-FREE VEGETABLE-OIL SPREAD (60% TO 70% OIL)
1 CUP WHITE WHOLE-WHEAT FLOUR	
½ TEASPOON BAKING POWDER	1 LARGE EGG
¼ TEASPOON SALT	2 TEASPOONS VANILLA EXTRACT
1 CUP SUGAR	

1 On sheet of waxed paper, combine all-purpose and whole-wheat flours, baking powder, and salt.
2 In large bowl, with mixer on low speed, beat sugar and vegetable oil spread until blended. Increase speed to high; beat until light and creamy, about 3 minutes, occasionally scraping down bowl with rubber spatula. Reduce speed to low; beat in egg and vanilla, then beat in flour mixture just until blended.
3 Divide dough in half; flatten each half into a disk. Wrap each disk with plastic wrap and refrigerate until dough is firm enough to roll, about 2 hours.
4 Preheat oven to 375°F.
5 On lightly floured surface, with floured rolling pin, roll one piece of dough ⅛ inch thick. With 2-inch cookie cutters, cut out as many cookies as possible; wrap and refrigerate trimmings. With lightly floured spatula, place cookies, 1 inch apart, on ungreased cookie sheet.
6 Bake cookies until lightly browned, 10 to 12 minutes. With thin metal spatula, transfer cookies to wire rack to cool. Repeat with remaining dough and trimmings.

EACH COOKIE: ABOUT 35 CALORIES | 1G PROTEIN | 5G CARBOHYDRATE | 1G TOTAL FAT (0G SATURATED) | 0G FIBER | 3MG CHOLESTEROL | 20MG SODIUM

CLASSIC SUGAR COOKIES

Here's the perfect, all-purpose sugar cookie dough. You can slice it into diamonds with a knife and sprinkle with colored sugar or cut it into shapes with cookie cutters and decorate with frosting. For a pretty dessert, press the dough into a tart shape, bake it, then fill the shell with berries and cream.

ACTIVE TIME: 1 HOUR 30 MINUTES PLUS CHILLING · **BAKE TIME:** 12 MINUTES PER BATCH

MAKES: 76 COOKIES

---

3 CUPS ALL-PURPOSE FLOUR	1½ CUPS SUGAR
½ TEASPOON BAKING POWDER	2 LARGE EGGS
½ TEASPOON SALT	1 TEASPOON VANILLA EXTRACT
1 CUP BUTTER (2 STICKS), SOFTENED (DO NOT USE MARGARINE)	ORNAMENTAL FROSTING (OPTIONAL, PAGE 15)

1 In large bowl, combine flour, baking powder, and salt. In separate large bowl, with mixer at low speed, beat butter and sugar until blended. Increase speed to high; beat until light and fluffy, about 5 minutes. Reduce speed to low; beat in eggs and vanilla until mixed, then beat in flour mixture just until blended, occasionally scraping bowl with rubber spatula. Divide dough into 4 equal pieces; flatten each into a disk. Wrap each disk in plastic and refrigerate overnight.

2 Preheat oven to 350°F. On lightly floured surface, with floured rolling pin, roll 1 piece of dough until slightly less than ¼ inch thick; keep remaining dough refrigerated. With floured 3- to 4-inch cookie cutters, cut dough into as many cookies as possible; reserve trimmings. Place cookies, 1 inch apart, on two ungreased large cookie sheets.

3 Bake until edges are golden, 12 to 15 minutes, rotating cookie sheets between upper and lower oven racks halfway through baking. With wide metal spatula, transfer cookies to wire racks to cool completely. Decorate with Ornamental Frosting, if desired.

4 Repeat with remaining dough and trimmings.

EACH COOKIE: ABOUT 60 CALORIES | 1G PROTEIN | 8G CARBOHYDRATE | 3G TOTAL FAT (2G SATURATED) | 0G FIBER | 13MG CHOLESTEROL | 47MG SODIUM

BROWN SUGAR CUT-OUT COOKIES

This buttery brown sugar dough is especially easy to roll and cut out. You can give the cookies a quick sprinkle with granulated sugar before baking, or frost and decorate them after they have baked and cooled.

ACTIVE TIME: 35 MINUTES PLUS CHILLING · **BAKE TIME:** 10 MINUTES PER BATCH
MAKES: 76 COOKIES

---

2 CUPS ALL-PURPOSE FLOUR	¾ CUP PACKED LIGHT BROWN SUGAR
½ TEASPOON BAKING SODA	1 LARGE EGG
¼ TEASPOON SALT	¼ CUP GRANULATED SUGAR, OR ORNAMENTAL FROSTING (SEE PAGE 15)
½ CUP BUTTER OR MARGARINE (1 STICK), SOFTENED	

1 Preheat oven to 350°F. In medium bowl, stir together flour, baking soda, and salt.

2 In large bowl, with mixer at medium speed, beat butter and brown sugar until combined. Reduce speed to low and beat in egg until blended. Beat in flour mixture until combined, scraping bowl occasionally with rubber spatula.

3 Shape dough into 2 balls; flatten each slightly. Wrap 1 ball in waxed paper and refrigerate while working with remaining half.

4 On lightly floured surface, with floured rolling pin, roll 1 ball of dough ⅛ inch thick. With floured 2-inch cookie cutters, cut out as many cookies as possible; reserve trimmings. Place cookies, about ½ inch apart, on ungreased large cookie sheet.

5 Sprinkle granulated sugar over cookies, if desired, or bake without sugar and frost when cool. Bake until edges begin to brown, 10 minutes. With wide metal spatula, transfer cookies to wire rack to cool completely.

6 Repeat with remaining dough, trimmings, and granulated sugar, if using.

EACH COOKIE: ABOUT 35 CALORIES | 0G PROTEIN | 5G CARBOHYDRATE | 1G TOTAL FAT (1G SATURATED) | 0G FIBER | 6MG CHOLESTEROL | 30 MG SODIUM

SOUR-CREAM CUT-OUT COOKIES

A sprinkle of sugar makes these beautiful cookies sparkle. When you re-roll the trimmings, press the pieces together to make a flattened rectangle rather than kneading them together—the cookies will be more tender.

ACTIVE TIME: 35 MINUTES PLUS CHILLING · **BAKE TIME:** 8 MINUTES PER BATCH

MAKES: 76 COOKIES

1¾ CUPS ALL-PURPOSE FLOUR

½ TEASPOON BAKING SODA

¼ TEASPOON SALT

½ CUP BUTTER OR MARGARINE (1 STICK), SOFTENED

1 CUP PLUS ABOUT 2 TABLESPOONS SUGAR

1 LARGE EGG

1 TEASPOON VANILLA EXTRACT

½ CUP SOUR CREAM

1 In medium bowl, stir together flour, baking soda, and salt. In large bowl, with mixer at medium speed, beat butter and 1 cup sugar until combined. Reduce speed to low and beat in egg and vanilla until blended. Beat in sour cream. Beat in flour mixture until combined, scraping bowl occasionally with rubber spatula.

2 Divide dough into 4 balls; flatten each slightly. Wrap each in waxed paper and refrigerate until dough is firm enough to roll, at least 2 hours or overnight. (If using margarine, refrigerate overnight.)

3 Preheat oven to 350°F. On lightly floured surface, with floured rolling pin, roll 1 piece of dough ⅛ inch thick, keeping remaining dough refrigerated. With floured 2-inch cookie cutters, cut out as many cookies as possible; reserve trimmings. Place cookies, about 1½ inches apart, on ungreased large cookie sheet. Sprinkle with some of remaining sugar.

4 Bake 8 minutes. With wide metal spatula, transfer cookies to wire racks to cool completely.

5 Repeat with remaining dough, trimmings, and sugar.

EACH COOKIE: ABOUT 35 CALORIES | 0G PROTEIN | 5G CARBOHYDRATE | 2G TOTAL FAT (1G SATURATED) | 0G FIBER | 7MG CHOLESTEROL | 30MG SODIUM

LEMON HEARTS

These delicate heart-shaped cookies are a charming accompaniment to tea or a sweet gift for a dear friend.

ACTIVE TIME: 40 MINUTES PLUS COOLING · **BAKE TIME:** 15 MINUTES PER BATCH
MAKES: 72 COOKIES

LEMON COOKIES

3 CUPS ALL-PURPOSE FLOUR

3 TABLESPOONS CORNSTARCH

¾ TEASPOON SALT

1½ CUPS BUTTER (3 STICKS), SOFTENED (DO NOT USE MARGARINE)

1 CUP CONFECTIONERS' SUGAR

1 TABLESPOON FRESHLY GRATED LEMON PEEL

1½ TEASPOONS LEMON EXTRACT

¼ TEASPOON ALMOND EXTRACT

LEMON GLAZE

1½ CUPS CONFECTIONERS' SUGAR

4 TO 5 TEASPOONS FRESH LEMON JUICE

1½ TEASPOONS FRESHLY GRATED LEMON PEEL

1 Prepare cookies: Preheat oven to 325°F. In medium bowl, whisk flour, cornstarch, and salt until blended.

2 In separate large bowl, with mixer at medium speed, beat butter and sugar until creamy, occasionally scraping bowl with rubber spatula. Beat in lemon peel and lemon and almond extracts. Reduce speed to low; gradually beat in flour mixture until blended, occasionally scraping bowl.

3 Divide dough in half. Between two 20-inch sheets of waxed paper, roll half of dough ⅜ inch thick. (If paper wrinkles during rolling, peel it off, gently pull to remove wrinkles, and reposition it.) With floured 2¼-inch heart-shaped cookie cutter, cut dough into as many cookies as possible. With floured ¾-inch heart-shaped cookie cutter, cut out and remove centers from cookies. Reserve centers and trimmings to reroll. With lightly floured wide spatula, carefully place cookies, 1 inch apart, on two ungreased large cookie sheets. (If dough becomes too soft to transfer to cookie sheet, freeze 10 minutes until firm.)

4 Bake cookies until edges are golden, 15 to 16 minutes, rotating cookie sheets between upper and lower racks halfway through baking. Transfer cookies to wire rack; cool 10 minutes.

5 Meanwhile, prepare glaze: In small bowl, with wire whisk or fork, mix confectioners' sugar, lemon juice, and lemon peel until blended. Dip top side of each warm cookie into glaze. Place cookies on wire rack set over waxed paper to catch any drips. Allow glaze to set, about 20 minutes.

6 Repeat with remaining dough, reserved centers, trimmings, and glaze, adding a little water to glaze if it begins to thicken.

EACH COOKIE: ABOUT 75 CALORIES | 1G PROTEIN | 9G CARBOHYDRATE | 4G TOTAL FAT
(3G SATURATED) | 0G FIBER | 11MG CHOLESTEROL | 65MG SODIUM

JELLY CENTERS

A dainty dollop of raspberry preserves sandwiched between two buttery cookies—what could be more delectable than that?

ACTIVE TIME: 45 MINUTES PLUS CHILLING AND COOLING · **BAKE TIME:** 10 MINUTES PER BATCH
MAKES: 54 SANDWICH COOKIES

1 CUP BUTTER OR MARGARINE (2 STICKS), SOFTENED	3 CUPS ALL-PURPOSE FLOUR
1¼ CUPS SUGAR	⅒ TEASPOON BAKING POWDER
2 LARGE EGGS, SEPARATED	⅛ TEASPOON SALT
2 TEASPOONS VANILLA EXTRACT	ABOUT 1 CUP SEEDLESS RASPBERRY PRESERVES

1 In large bowl, with mixer at low speed, beat butter and 1 cup sugar until blended, occasionally scraping bowl with rubber spatula. Increase speed to high; beat until light and fluffy, about 3 minutes. At low speed, beat in egg yolks and vanilla until blended. Gradually beat in flour, baking powder, and salt. Shape dough into 2 balls; flatten each slightly. Wrap each ball in plastic and refrigerate until firm enough to roll, 1 hour.

2 Preheat oven to 350°F. Between two sheets of floured waxed paper, roll one piece of dough ⅛ inch thick; keep remaining dough refrigerated. With floured 2-inch cookie cutter (we like rounds or stars), cut out as many cookies as possible. Place cookies, about ½ inch apart, on two ungreased large cookie sheets; reserve trimmings. With ½-inch round or star-shaped cookie cutter, cut out centers from half of cookies. Remove centers; add to trimmings.

3 In cup, with fork, beat egg whites slightly. With pastry brush, brush cookies with cut-out centers with some egg white, then sprinkle with some of the remaining ¼ cup sugar. Bake all cookies until lightly browned, 10 to 12 minutes, rotating cookie sheets between upper and lower oven racks halfway through baking. With wide metal spatula, transfer cookies to wire rack to cool.

4 Repeat Steps 2 and 3 with trimmings and remaining dough.

5 When cookies are cool, spread center of each cookie without cut-out center with ¼ to ½ teaspoon preserves; top each with a cookie with a cut-out center, gently pressing cookies together to form a sandwich.

EACH COOKIE: ABOUT 95 CALORIES | 1G PROTEIN | 14G CARBOHYDRATE | 4G TOTAL FAT (1G SATURATED) | 0G FIBER | 8MG CHOLESTEROL | 55MG SODIUM

LEMON-GLAZED FLOWERS

You'll need a scalloped cookie cutter to create these pretty glazed flower cookies. You don't have to bake the whole recipe at once; the dough can be frozen for up to three months.

ACTIVE TIME: 45 MINUTES PLUS CHILLING · **BAKE TIME:** 10 MINUTES PER BATCH
MAKES: 108 COOKIES

BUTTER COOKIES

1½ CUPS BUTTER OR MARGARINE
    (3 STICKS), SOFTENED

1⅓ CUPS GRANULATED SUGAR

½   TEASPOON SALT

3   LARGE EGGS

4½ CUPS ALL-PURPOSE FLOUR

LEMON GLAZE

1½ CUPS CONFECTIONERS' SUGAR

¼   CUP PLUS 1 TEASPOON FRESH LEMON
    JUICE (FROM 1 TO 2 LEMONS)

1   Prepare cookies: In large bowl, with mixer at low speed, beat butter, granulated sugar, and salt until blended. Increase speed to high; beat until creamy. At low speed, beat in eggs, one at a time, beating well after each addition. Gradually beat in flour just until blended.
2   Divide dough into 4 equal pieces; flatten each into a disk. Wrap each disk in plastic and refrigerate until dough is firm enough to roll, at least 2 hours.
3   Meanwhile, prepare glaze: In small bowl, whisk confectioners' sugar and lemon juice until smooth; cover and set aside.
4   Preheat oven to 350°F. On lightly floured surface, with floured rolling pin, roll 1 piece of dough ⅛ inch thick. With floured 2½-inch round scalloped cookie cutter, cut dough into as many cookies as possible; wrap and refrigerate trimmings. With floured wide metal spatula, carefully place cookies, 1 inch apart, on ungreased large cookie sheet.
5   Bake cookies until lightly browned, 10 to 12 minutes. With wide metal spatula, transfer cookies to wire rack. Brush tops of warm cookies generously with glaze; cool on wire rack.
6   Repeat with remaining dough, trimmings, and glaze.

EACH COOKIE: ABOUT 60 CALORIES | 1G PROTEIN | 8G CARBOHYDRATE | 3G TOTAL FAT
(2G SATURATED) | 0G FIBER | 13MG CHOLESTEROL | 40MG SODIUM

FINNISH ALMOND COOKIES

The perfect partner for a cup of freshly brewed coffee, these crisp cookies are a Scandinavian favorite. Better yet, there's almost no fuss and muss because you roll them out, cut them into rectangles, and top them with sugar and almonds right on the baking sheet.

ACTIVE TIME: 25 MINUTES · **BAKE TIME:** 12 MINUTES PER BATCH
MAKES: 42 COOKIES

¾ CUP BUTTER OR MARGARINE (1½ STICKS), SOFTENED

¼ CUP PLUS 2 TABLESPOONS SUGAR

1 LARGE EGG, SEPARATED

1 TEASPOON ALMOND EXTRACT

2 CUPS ALL-PURPOSE FLOUR

1 TABLESPOON WATER (IF NECESSARY)

1 CUP SLICED BLANCHED ALMONDS (4 OUNCES)

1 Preheat oven to 375°F. In large bowl, with mixer at medium speed, beat butter and ¼ cup sugar until light and fluffy. Beat in egg yolk and almond extract until blended. Reduce speed to low; gradually beat in flour. If dough is dry and crumbly, sprinkle with water; beat just until blended. Divide dough in half.

2 Sprinkle large ungreased cookie sheet with flour (if your cookie sheet has a rim on four sides, use it upside down). With floured rolling pin, on cookie sheet, roll 1 piece of dough into 10½" by 9" rectangle. Lightly beat egg white. With pastry brush, brush dough with some egg white; sprinkle with half of almonds and 1 tablespoon sugar. Cut dough crosswise into seven 1½-inch-wide strips; cut each strip crosswise into 3 pieces.

3 Bake until edges are lightly browned, 12 to 15 minutes. If any cookies have not browned around edges, return to oven and bake several minutes longer. With wide metal spatula, transfer cookies to wire rack to cool completely.

4 Repeat with remaining dough, almonds, and sugar.

EACH COOKIE: ABOUT 75 CALORIES | 1G PROTEIN | 7G CARBOHYDRATE | 5G TOTAL FAT (2G SATURATED) | 0.5G FIBER | 14MG CHOLESTEROL | 35MG SODIUM

BUTTERSCOTCH FINGERS

When butter and brown sugar are combined, there's an almost magical transformation to the flavor we know as butterscotch. Here, chopped pecans accentuate the richness.

ACTIVE TIME: 30 MINUTES PLUS CHILLING · **BAKE TIME:** 12 MINUTES PER BATCH
MAKES: 96 COOKIES

2⅓ CUPS ALL-PURPOSE FLOUR	1 CUP PACKED DARK BROWN SUGAR
½ TEASPOON BAKING POWDER	1 TEASPOON VANILLA EXTRACT
½ TEASPOON SALT	1 LARGE EGG
1 CUP BUTTER OR MARGARINE (2 STICKS), SOFTENED	¾ CUP PECANS, CHOPPED

1 In medium bowl, combine flour, baking powder, and salt.

2 In large bowl, with mixer at medium speed, beat butter and sugar until creamy, occasionally scraping bowl with rubber spatula. Beat in vanilla, then egg. At low speed, gradually add flour mixture; beat just until blended, occasionally scraping bowl. With wooden spoon, stir in pecans.

3 Shape dough into a 12" by 3¾" by 1" brick. Wrap brick in plastic and refrigerate until firm enough to slice, at least 6 hours or overnight. Or place brick in freezer for about 2 hours. (If using margarine, freeze brick overnight.)

4 Preheat oven to 350°F. Grease large cookie sheet. With sharp knife, cut brick crosswise into ⅛-inch-thick slices. Place slices, 1 inch apart, on prepared cookie sheet. Bake until lightly browned around edges, 12 to 14 minutes. With wide metal spatula, transfer cookies to wire rack to cool.

5 Repeat with remaining dough.

EACH COOKIE: ABOUT 45 CALORIES | 1G PROTEIN | 5G CARBOHYDRATE | 3G TOTAL FAT (1G SATURATED) | 0G FIBER | 8MG CHOLESTEROL | 38MG SODIUM

PINWHEELS

You'll be surprised at how easy it is to shape these pretty treats. For more variety in both flavor and color, try using several different kinds of jam.

ACTIVE TIME: 35 MINUTES PLUS CHILLING · **BAKE TIME:** 9 MINUTES PER BATCH

MAKES: 24 COOKIES

1⅓ CUPS ALL-PURPOSE FLOUR	½ CUP SUGAR
¼ TEASPOON BAKING POWDER	1 LARGE EGG
⅛ TEASPOON SALT	1 TEASPOON VANILLA EXTRACT
6 TABLESPOONS BUTTER OR MARGARINE, SOFTENED	¼ CUP DAMSON PLUM, SEEDLESS RASPBERRY, OR OTHER JAM

1 In small bowl, stir together flour, baking powder, and salt.

2 In large bowl, with mixer at medium speed, beat butter and sugar until light and fluffy. Beat in egg and vanilla until combined. Reduce speed to low and beat in flour mixture just until combined. Divide dough in half. Wrap each half in waxed paper and refrigerate until firm enough to roll, at least 1 hour or overnight. (If using margarine, freeze overnight.)

3 Preheat oven to 375°F. On floured surface, with floured rolling pin, roll 1 piece of dough into 10 by 7½" rectangle; keep remaining dough refrigerated. With fluted pastry wheel or sharp knife, cut into twelve 2½-inch squares. Place 1 square at a time, 1 inch apart, on two ungreased cookie sheets. Make a 1½-inch cut from each corner toward center. Spoon ½ teaspoon jam in center of each square. Fold every other tip in to center. Repeat with remaining squares.

4 Bake until edges are lightly browned and cookies are set, 9 minutes, rotating sheets between upper and lower racks halfway through baking. With wide metal spatula, transfer to wire racks to cool completely.

5 Repeat with remaining dough and jam.

EACH COOKIE: ABOUT 80 CALORIES | 1G PROTEIN | 12G CARBOHYDRATE | 3G TOTAL FAT (2G SATURATED) | 0G FIBER | 17MG CHOLESTEROL | 50MG SODIUM

PFEFFERNUSSE

These tiny melt-in-your-mouth cookies have a spicy orange flavor. Although *Pfeffernusse* means "pepper nuts" in German, the cookies are more often spiced with cinnamon, cloves, and allspice, as they are here. This recipe makes an extra-big batch; reduce the yield if you don't need so many cookies, but remember, they are petite.

ACTIVE TIME: 1 HOUR 30 MINUTES PLUS CHILLING · **BAKE TIME:** 8 MINUTES PER BATCH
MAKES: 240 COOKIES

---

2 CUPS SUGAR	1 TEASPOON GROUND CINNAMON
3 LARGE EGGS	1 TEASPOON GROUND ALLSPICE
3½ CUPS ALL-PURPOSE FLOUR	1 TEASPOON BAKING POWDER
2 TABLESPOONS FRESHLY GRATED ORANGE PEEL	1 TEASPOON LEMON EXTRACT
	½ TEASPOON GROUND CLOVES

1 In large bowl, with mixer at low speed, beat sugar and eggs until blended. Increase speed to high; beat until creamy. Reduce speed to low; add flour, orange peel, cinnamon, allspice, baking powder, lemon extract, and cloves and beat until well combined, occasionally scraping bowl with rubber spatula.

2 With lightly floured hands, shape dough into 4 balls; flatten each slightly. Wrap each ball in plastic and refrigerate overnight. (Dough will be very sticky even after chilling.)

3 Preheat oven to 400°F. Grease large cookie sheet. On well-floured surface, with floured rolling pin, roll 1 piece of dough into 10" by 6" rectangle; keep remaining dough in refrigerator. With floured pastry wheel or sharp knife, cut dough lengthwise into 6 strips, then cut each strip crosswise into 10 pieces. Place cookies, about ½ inch apart, on prepared cookie sheet.

4 Bake until lightly browned, 8 to 10 minutes. With wide metal spatula, transfer cookies to wire racks to cool.

5 Repeat with remaining dough.

EACH COOKIE: ABOUT 15 CALORIES | 0G PROTEIN | 3G CARBOHYDRATE | 0G TOTAL FAT (0G SATURATED) | 0G FIBER | 4MG CHOLESTEROL | 5MG SODIUM

SPICE THINS

These crisp, buttery cookies originated in Sweden. The family-size recipe makes almost eight dozen cookies, but they keep very, very well.

ACTIVE TIME: 45 MINUTES PLUS CHILLING · **BAKE TIME:** 10 MINUTES PER BATCH
MAKES: 90 COOKIES

1 CUP BUTTER (2 STICKS), SOFTENED (DO NOT USE MARGARINE)	2½ TEASPOONS BAKING SODA
1 CUP SUGAR	2 TEASPOONS GROUND CINNAMON
½ CUP DARK CORN SYRUP	2 TEASPOONS GROUND CLOVES
½ CUP HEAVY OR WHIPPING CREAM	2 TEASPOONS GROUND GINGER
	4 CUPS ALL-PURPOSE FLOUR

1 In large bowl, with mixer at low speed, beat butter and sugar until blended. Increase speed to high; beat until light and creamy, occasionally scraping bowl with rubber spatula. Reduce speed to low; beat in corn syrup, cream, baking soda, cinnamon, cloves, and ginger until blended. Gradually beat in flour until well mixed.

2 Divide dough into 8 pieces. Wrap each piece in plastic and refrigerate overnight.

3 Preheat oven to 350°F. On lightly floured surface, with floured rolling pin, roll 1 piece of dough ⅛ inch thick, keeping remaining dough refrigerated. With floured 3-inch round fluted cookie cutter, cut dough into as many cookies as possible; reserve trimmings. Place cookies, 1 inch apart, on ungreased large cookie sheet.

4 Bake until lightly browned, 10 to 12 minutes. With wide metal spatula, transfer cookies to wire rack to cool.

5 Repeat with remaining dough and trimmings.

EACH COOKIE: ABOUT 55 CALORIES | 1G PROTEIN | 8G CARBOHYDRATE | 3G TOTAL FAT (2G SATURATED) | 0G FIBER | 7MG CHOLESTEROL | 60MG SODIUM

CINNAMON TWISTS

These tender cream-cheese cookies are coated with walnut-cinnamon sugar before they are twisted and baked.

ACTIVE TIME: 1 HOUR PLUS CHILLING · **BAKE TIME:** 15 MINUTES PER BATCH

MAKES: 66 COOKIES

1 PACKAGE (8 OUNCES) CREAM CHEESE, SOFTENED	¾ CUP WALNUTS
	1 CUP SUGAR
1 CUP MARGARINE OR BUTTER (2 STICKS), SOFTENED	2 TEASPOONS GROUND CINNAMON
2½ CUPS ALL-PURPOSE FLOUR	1 LARGE EGG, BEATEN

1 In large bowl, with mixer at low speed, beat cream cheese and butter until blended, constantly scraping bowl with rubber spatula. Increase speed to high; beat until light and creamy, about 2 minutes. With mixer at low speed, gradually add 1 cup flour and beat until blended. With wooden spoon, stir in remaining 1½ cups flour until smooth.

2 On lightly floured sheet of plastic wrap, pat dough into 9-inch square. Wrap and refrigerate until dough is firm enough to roll, 2 hours.

3 Meanwhile, in food processor with knife blade attached, process nuts and ¼ cup sugar until walnuts are finely ground. In small bowl, stir cinnamon, remaining sugar, and nut mixture until blended; set aside.

4 Preheat oven to 400°F. Grease large cookie sheet. On lightly floured sheet of waxed paper, with floured rolling pin, roll dough square into 11" by 10½" rectangle. With pastry brush, brush some beaten egg over top of dough rectangle. Sprinkle with half of walnut mixture; gently press walnut mixture into dough. Invert dough rectangle onto another sheet of lightly floured waxed paper, nut side down. Brush with beaten egg, sprinkle with remaining walnut mixture, and gently press nut mixture into dough.

5 Cut dough lengthwise into three 3½-inch-wide bars, then cut bars crosswise into ½-inch-wide strips to make sixty-six 3½-inch-long strips. Twist each strip twice, then place, about 1 inch apart, on cookie sheet.

6 Bake twists until lightly browned, 15 to 17 minutes. With wide metal spatula, gently loosen from cookie sheet; transfer to wire rack to cool.

7 Repeat with remaining strips.

EACH COOKIE: ABOUT 75 CALORIES | 1G PROTEIN | 7G CARBOHYDRATE | 5G TOTAL FAT (1G SATURATED) | 0G FIBER | 7MG CHOLESTEROL | 50MG SODIUM

BISCOCHITOS

These flaky, rich Mexican cookies are traditionally made with lard. We substituted half butter and half shortening, with delicious results.

ACTIVE TIME: 18 MINUTES · **BAKE TIME:** 11 MINUTES PER BATCH
MAKES: 76 COOKIES

3	CUPS ALL-PURPOSE FLOUR	1	CUP SUGAR
1½	TEASPOONS BAKING POWDER	2	TEASPOONS ANISE SEEDS
¼	TEASPOON SALT	1	LARGE EGG YOLK
½	CUP BUTTER OR MARGARINE (1 STICK), SOFTENED	¼	CUP SHERRY OR SWEET WINE
½	CUP VEGETABLE SHORTENING	4	TEASPOONS GROUND CINNAMON

1 Preheat oven to 375°F. In large bowl, stir together flour, baking powder, and salt.

2 In separate large bowl, with mixer at medium speed, beat butter, shortening, and ½ cup sugar until light and fluffy. Beat in anise seeds and egg yolk until well combined. Beat in sherry until smooth. Reduce speed to low and beat in flour mixture until well combined.

3 Divide dough into 4 equal pieces. On lightly floured surface, roll out one piece of dough, ¼ inch thick.

4 In small bowl, stir together remaining ½ cup sugar and cinnamon. Sprinkle one-fourth of cinnamon-sugar mixture over dough. With 2-inch decorative cookie cutter, cut out as many cookies as possible, making them very close to each other; do not reroll scraps.

5 Place cookies, 1 inch apart, on two ungreased large cookie sheets. Bake until set, 11 minutes, rotating sheets between upper and lower racks halfway through baking. Cool on cookie sheets on wire racks 1 minute. With wide metal spatula, transfer to wire racks to cool completely.

6 Repeat with remaining dough and cinnamon-sugar.

EACH COOKIE: ABOUT 50 CALORIES | 1G PROTEIN | 6G CARBOHYDRATE | 3G TOTAL FAT (1G SATURATED) | 0G FIBER | 6MG CHOLESTEROL | 30MG SODIUM

SOUR-CREAM NUT ROLLS

These festive yeast rolls feature a rich sour cream dough and a walnut-and-sugar filling. For convenience, you can raise the shaped rolls in the refrigerator overnight.

ACTIVE TIME: 50 MINUTES PLUS STANDING AND COOLING · **BAKE TIME:** 40 MINUTES
MAKES: 48 COOKIES

WALNUT FILLING

- 2½ CUPS WALNUTS, TOASTED (SEE OPPOSITE) AND COOLED
- ¾ CUP SUGAR
- 2 TABLESPOONS BUTTER OR MARGARINE, MELTED
- 1 TABLESPOON VANILLA EXTRACT
- 2 TEASPOONS FRESHLY GRATED ORANGE PEEL
- ¼ TEASPOON SALT

SOUR-CREAM DOUGH

- ¼ CUP WARM WATER (105° TO 115°F)
- 1 PACKAGE ACTIVE DRY YEAST
- 1 TEASPOON PLUS ¼ CUP SUGAR
- 3 CUPS ALL-PURPOSE FLOUR
- ¾ TEASPOON SALT
- ½ CUP BUTTER OR MARGARINE (1 STICK), MELTED
- ½ CUP SOUR CREAM
- 2 LARGE EGGS

1 Prepare filling: In food processor with knife blade attached, process walnuts, sugar, butter, vanilla, orange peel, and salt until walnuts are finely ground; set aside.

2 Prepare dough: In small bowl, combine warm water, yeast, and 1 teaspoon sugar; let stand until foamy, about 5 minutes.

3 In large bowl, stir together flour, remaining ¼ cup sugar, and salt. Stir in butter, sour cream, 1 whole egg, 1 egg yolk, and yeast mixture until evenly moistened. (Cover and refrigerate remaining egg white.) With floured hands, knead dough in bowl a few times until dough comes together (dough will be sticky). Cover bowl with plastic wrap; let stand 10 minutes.

4 Divide dough in half. On lightly floured surface, with floured rolling pin, roll 1 piece of dough into 14" by 12" rectangle. Sprinkle half of filling evenly over dough; gently press into dough.

5 Starting from one long side of dough rectangle, tightly roll dough jelly-roll fashion. Place roll, seam side down, on one side of ungreased large cookie sheet. Repeat with remaining dough and filling. Place second roll, 4 inches from first roll, on same cookie sheet. Cover rolls with plastic wrap and let rise in warm place (80° to 85°F) 1 hour. If you like, refrigerate rolls, on cookie sheet, overnight instead. When ready to bake, let stand at room temperature 30 minutes before completing Steps 6 through 8.

6 Preheat oven to 325°F. Bake rolls 35 minutes.

7 Meanwhile in cup, lightly beat reserved egg white. Brush rolls with egg white. Bake until golden, 5 minutes longer. With wide metal spatula, transfer rolls to wire rack to cool completely.

8 When rolls are cool, with serrated knife, cut crosswise into ½-inch-thick slices.

EACH COOKIE: ABOUT 115 CALORIES | 2G PROTEIN | 11G CARBOHYDRATE | 7G TOTAL FAT (2G SATURATED) | 1G FIBER | 17MG CHOLESTEROL | 80MG SODIUM

TOASTING NUTS

An easy way to make your cookies taste even more delicious is to toast the nuts.

- Preheat oven to 350°F. (If you aren't heating the oven for baking, you can use a toaster oven instead.)

- Spread out the nuts in a single layer on a rimmed baking sheet or pan; place on the middle rack in your oven.

- Heat until lightly browned, 10 to 15 minutes, stirring occasionally so nuts in the center of the pan are moved to the edges, where they will brown faster.

- Immediately transfer nuts to a cool platter or baking pan to reduce their temperature and stop the browning. See Tip.

- If you're toasting just a few nuts, heat them in a dry skillet over low heat for 3 to 5 minutes, stirring frequently.

TIP To remove the bitter skins from hazelnuts, toast them as directed above until any portions without skin begin to brown. Transfer the nuts to a clean, dry kitchen towel and rub them until the skins come off.

APRICOT-RASPBERRY RUGELACH

Here, we give classic rugelach a new twist.

ACTIVE TIME: 1 HOUR PLUS CHILLING · **BAKE TIME:** 35 MINUTES
MAKES: 48 RUGELACH

---

1 CUP BUTTER OR MARGARINE
(2 STICKS), SOFTENED

1 PACKAGE (8 OUNCES) CREAM CHEESE,
SOFTENED

¾ CUP GRANULATED SUGAR

1 TEASPOON VANILLA EXTRACT

¼ TEASPOON SALT

2 CUPS ALL-PURPOSE FLOUR

1 CUP WALNUTS (4 OUNCES), CHOPPED

¾ CUP DRIED APRICOTS, CHOPPED

¼ CUP PACKED LIGHT BROWN SUGAR

1½ TEASPOONS GROUND CINNAMON

½ CUP SEEDLESS RASPBERRY PRESERVES

1 TABLESPOON MILK

1 In large bowl, with mixer at low speed, beat butter and cream cheese until creamy. Beat in ¼ cup granulated sugar, vanilla, and salt. Beat in 1 cup flour. With wooden spoon, stir in remaining 1 cup flour just until blended. Divide dough into 4 equal pieces; flatten each into a disk. Wrap each disk in waxed paper and refrigerate until firm, at least 2 hours.

2 Preheat oven to 325°F. Line two large cookie sheets with foil; grease foil.

3 In medium bowl, combine walnuts, apricots, brown sugar, ¼ cup plus 2 tablespoons granulated sugar, and ½ teaspoon cinnamon until well mixed.

4 On lightly floured surface, with floured rolling pin, roll 1 disk of dough into 9-inch round; keep remaining dough refrigerated. Spread 2 table-spoons preserves over dough. Sprinkle with ½ cup apricot mixture; gently press to adhere. Cut dough into 12 equal wedges and roll up each wedge, jelly-roll fashion. Place rugelach, point side down, ½ inch apart, on prepared cookie sheets; shape into crescents. (See Cutting & Shaping Rugelach, opposite.) Repeat with remaining dough.

5 In cup, combine remaining 2 tablespoons granulated sugar and remaining 1 teaspoon cinnamon. With pastry brush, brush rugelach with milk. Sprinkle evenly with cinnamon-sugar.

6 Bake until golden, 35 to 40 minutes, rotating cookie sheets between upper and lower oven racks halfway through baking. With wide metal spatula, immediately transfer rugelach to wire racks to cool completely.

EACH COOKIE: ABOUT 115 CALORIES | 1G PROTEIN | 12G CARBOHYDRATE | 7G TOTAL FAT (4G SATURATED) | 0.5G FIBER | 16MG CHOLESTEROL | 67MG SODIUM

CUTTING & SHAPING RUGELACH

Step 1: After spreading the filling on rugelach dough, cut into wedges using a pastry wheel or a sharp knife.

Step 2: Starting from wide end, roll up rugelach wedges. Place with the point down and shape into a crescent.

SHAPED & ICEBOX COOKIES

Shaped, sliced, curled, or twisted—molded cookies are almost as much fun to make as they are to eat.

Many of the cookies in this chapter have traditions of long standing. Carried to America from a variety of homelands, they now appear together in cookie tins across the country, especially at the holidays. Icebox or refrigerator cookies became the "rage"—and the first convenience food—in the late nineteenth century, when women discovered that having a roll of cookie dough in the icebox meant they could bake and serve warm cookies at a moment's notice. This time-saver is just as useful today.

Although these are a little trickier than drop cookies, you should be able to get delicious results if you follow these easy tips.

- **Work quickly with each ball of dough.** You can start shaping the dough as soon as it is made because molded cookie dough is usually stiff enough so that it doesn't require chilling. But move fast so that the heat of your hands doesn't melt the butter in it and make it sticky.
- **If the dough begins to stick to your hands,** rubbing them with a little flour or vegetable oil will help.
- **If the dough starts to get crumbly,** moisten your hands with water. It will make the cookies easier to shape.
- **Follow cookie press directions carefully,** especially when making spritz cookies, as all of them have slightly different instructions.
- **To freeze dough,** just wrap it tightly in heavy-duty foil, pack in an airtight container, and label it with the contents and date. It will keep for three months. Be sure to thaw the dough in the refrigerator.

Almond Macaroon Fingers (page 94)

MOLASSES COOKIES

An old-time favorite. Everyone will enjoy rolling the spicy dough into balls and dipping them in sugar.

ACTIVE TIME: 40 MINUTES PLUS CHILLING · **BAKE TIME:** 10 MINUTES PER BATCH
MAKES: 72 COOKIES

¾ CUP BUTTER OR MARGARINE (1½ STICKS)

¼ CUP LIGHT (MILD) MOLASSES

1¼ CUPS SUGAR

1 LARGE EGG

2 CUPS ALL-PURPOSE FLOUR

2 TEASPOONS BAKING SODA

1 TEASPOON GROUND CINNAMON

½ TEASPOON GROUND GINGER

½ TEASPOON SALT

¼ TEASPOON GROUND CLOVES

1 Preheat oven to 375°F. In 3-quart saucepan, melt butter over low heat. Remove saucepan from heat and, with wire whisk, beat in molasses and 1 cup sugar until blended; whisk in egg. With wooden spoon, stir in flour, baking soda, cinnamon, ginger, salt, and cloves until mixed. Transfer dough to medium bowl and freeze until firm enough to handle, about 15 minutes.
2 Spread remaining ¼ cup sugar on sheet of waxed paper. Roll dough into 1-inch balls; roll balls in sugar to coat. Place balls, 2½ inches apart, on ungreased large cookie sheet.
3 Bake until cookies spread and darken, 10 to 12 minutes. Cool on cookie sheet on wire rack 1 minute, then transfer cookies to wire rack to cool completely.
4 Repeat with remaining dough.

EACH COOKIE: ABOUT 45 CALORIES | 1G PROTEIN | 7G CARBOHYDRATE | 2G TOTAL FAT (0G SATURATED) | 0G FIBER | 3MG CHOLESTEROL | 75MG SODIUM

JUMBO GINGERSNAPS

We like our soft, chewy gingersnaps extra big, but you can make them smaller if you prefer. Be sure to cool the cookies briefly on the cookie sheet before moving them to racks, as they are very moist when hot and could fall apart.

ACTIVE TIME: 20 MINUTES · **BAKE TIME:** 15 MINUTES

MAKES: 10 GIANT COOKIES OR 30 SMALL COOKIES

2   CUPS ALL-PURPOSE FLOUR

2   TEASPOONS GROUND GINGER

1   TEASPOON BAKING SODA

½   TEASPOON GROUND CINNAMON

½   TEASPOON SALT

¼   TEASPOON GROUND BLACK PEPPER (OPTIONAL)

¾   CUP VEGETABLE SHORTENING

½   CUP PLUS 2 TABLESPOONS SUGAR

1   LARGE EGG

½   CUP DARK MOLASSES

1   Preheat oven to 350°F. In medium bowl, combine flour, ginger, baking soda, cinnamon, salt, and pepper, if using.

2   In large bowl, with mixer at medium speed, beat shortening and ½ cup sugar until light and fluffy. Beat in egg until blended; beat in molasses. Reduce speed to low; beat in flour mixture just until blended.

3   Place remaining 2 tablespoons sugar on sheet of waxed paper. Roll ¼ cup dough into ball; roll in sugar to coat evenly. Repeat with remaining dough to make 10 balls in all. Place balls, 3 inches apart, on ungreased large cookie sheet. Or, for small cookies, roll dough by slightly rounded table-spoons into balls and place 2 inches apart on two ungreased cookie sheets.

4   Bake until set, about 15 minutes for large cookies or 9 to 11 minutes for smaller cookies, rotating cookie sheets between upper and lower oven racks halfway through baking. Cookies will be very soft and may appear moist in cracks. Cool 1 minute on cookie sheets on wire racks; with wide metal spatula, transfer cookies to wire racks to cool completely.

EACH GIANT COOKIE: ABOUT 325 CALORIES | 3G PROTEIN | 42G CARBOHYDRATE | 5G TOTAL FAT (1G SATURATED) | 0G FIBER | 7MG CHOLESTEROL | 86MG SODIUM

EACH SMALL COOKIE: ABOUT 108 CALORIES | 1G PROTEIN | 14G CARBOHYDRATE | 16G TOTAL FAT (4G SATURATED) | 1G FIBER | 21MG CHOLESTEROL | 28MG SODIUM

SNICKERDOODLES

Despite their funny name, these cinnamon sugar–coated butter cookies are now considered an American classic. They are so much fun to make, the kids will beg to help.

ACTIVE TIME: 25 MINUTES · **BAKE TIME:** 12 MINUTES PER BATCH
MAKES: 54 COOKIES

3 CUPS ALL-PURPOSE FLOUR	1⅓ CUPS PLUS ¼ CUP SUGAR
2 TEASPOONS CREAM OF TARTAR	2 LARGE EGGS
1 TEASPOON BAKING SODA	1 TEASPOON VANILLA EXTRACT
1 CUP BUTTER OR MARGARINE (2 STICKS), SOFTENED	1½ TEASPOONS GROUND CINNAMON

1 Preheat oven to 375°F. In large bowl, stir together flour, cream of tartar, and baking soda.

2 In separate large bowl, with mixer at medium speed, beat butter and 1⅓ cups sugar until light and fluffy. Beat in eggs and vanilla. Reduce speed to low; beat in flour mixture until well blended.

3 In small bowl, combine cinnamon and remaining ¼ cup sugar. With hands, shape dough into 1-inch balls. Roll in cinnamon-sugar to coat. Place balls, 1 inch apart, on ungreased large cookie sheet. Bake until set and lightly golden and slightly crinkly on top, 12 minutes. Cool on cookie sheet on wire rack 1 minute. With wide metal spatula, transfer cookies to wire racks to cool completely.

4 Repeat with remaining dough.

EACH COOKIE: ABOUT 80 CALORIES | 1G PROTEIN | 11G CARBOHYDRATE | 4G TOTAL FAT (2G SATURATED) | 0G FIBER | 17MG CHOLESTEROL | 60MG SODIUM

THUMBPRINT COOKIES

We dolloped these cookies with homemade blueberry jam, but raspberry or strawberry would be equally good.

ACTIVE TIME: 40 MINUTES · **BAKE TIME:** 20 MINUTES PER BATCH
MAKES: 56 COOKIES

2 LARGE EGGS	½ TEASPOON ALMOND EXTRACT
¾ CUP BUTTER OR MARGARINE (1½ STICKS), SOFTENED	¼ TEASPOON SALT
	2 CUPS ALL-PURPOSE FLOUR
¾ CUP SUGAR	1¼ CUPS WALNUTS, FINELY CHOPPED
½ TEASPOON VANILLA EXTRACT	½ CUP FAVORITE JAM

1 Preheat oven to 350°F. Grease large cookie sheet.
2 In large bowl, with fork, beat eggs lightly. Measure out 3 tablespoons beaten egg and transfer to small bowl for later use.
3 Add butter, sugar, vanilla and almond extracts, and salt to eggs in large bowl. With mixer at medium speed, beat until evenly mixed, occasionally scraping bowl with rubber spatula. Add flour and stir just until blended.
4 Divide dough into 4 equal pieces. Divide each piece into 14 pieces and shape into balls. Spread walnuts on a sheet of waxed paper. Dip balls in reserved egg, then roll in walnuts, gently pressing nuts into dough.
5 Place balls, 2 inches apart, on prepared cookie sheet. With thumb, make small indentation in center of each ball. Bake until golden, 20 minutes. Transfer cookies to wire rack. Immediately fill each indentation with a rounded ½ teaspoon of jam. Cool cookies completely on wire rack.
6 Repeat with remaining balls and jam.

EACH COOKIE: ABOUT 90 CALORIES | 1G PROTEIN | 10G CARBOHYDRATE | 5G TOTAL FAT (1G SATURATED) | 0.5G FIBER | 9MG CHOLESTEROL | 55MG SODIUM

RASPBERRY LINZER COOKIES

Our hazelnut cookies topped with raspberry jam deliver all the flavor of the traditional Austrian linzer torte in a bite-size package.

ACTIVE TIME: 45 MINUTES · **BAKE TIME:** 20 MINUTES PER BATCH
MAKES: 48 COOKIES

1⅓ CUPS HAZELNUTS (FILBERTS, ABOUT 5.5 OUNCES)

½ CUP SUGAR

¾ CUP BUTTER OR MARGARINE (1½ STICKS), CUT INTO PIECES

1 TEASPOON VANILLA EXTRACT

¼ TEASPOON SALT

1¾ CUPS ALL-PURPOSE FLOUR

¼ CUP SEEDLESS RED-RASPBERRY JAM

1 Preheat oven to 350°F. Toast and skin 1 cup hazelnuts (see page 75); set aside remaining ⅓ cup.

2 In food processor with knife blade attached, process 1 cup hazelnuts and sugar until nuts are finely ground. Add butter, vanilla, and salt and process until blended. Add flour and process until evenly combined. Remove knife blade and press dough together with hands.

3 Finely chop remaining ⅓ cup hazelnuts; spread on sheet of waxed paper. With hands, shape dough into 1-inch balls (dough may be slightly crumbly). Roll balls in nuts, gently pressing nuts into dough. Place balls, about 1½ inches apart, on ungreased large cookie sheet.

4 With tip of spoon, make small indentation in center of each ball. Fill each indentation with ¼ teaspoon jam. Bake until lightly golden around edges, 20 minutes. With wide metal spatula, transfer cookies to wire racks to cool completely.

5 Repeat with remaining balls and jam.

EACH COOKIE: ABOUT 75 CALORIES | 1G PROTEIN | 7G CARBOHYDRATE | 5G TOTAL FAT (2G SATURATED) | 0.5G FIBER | 8MG CHOLESTEROL | 40MG SODIUM

CHOCOLATE CRINKLES

This cookie takes its name from its interesting shape. As the rich, sugar-coated dough bakes, it spreads into puffy rounds with small furrows. It makes a luscious addition to any lunch box or cookie tray.

ACTIVE TIME: 25 MINUTES PLUS CHILLING · **BAKE TIME:** 8 MINUTES PER BATCH
MAKES: 96 COOKIES

1¾ CUPS ALL-PURPOSE FLOUR

½ CUP UNSWEETENED COCOA

1 TEASPOON BAKING SODA

½ TEASPOON BAKING POWDER

¼ TEASPOON SALT

½ CUP BUTTER OR MARGARINE (1 STICK), SOFTENED

1¼ CUPS GRANULATED SUGAR

2 TABLESPOONS LIGHT CORN SYRUP

2 SQUARES (2 OUNCES) UNSWEETENED CHOCOLATE, MELTED AND COOLED

2 LARGE EGGS

2 TEASPOONS VANILLA EXTRACT

½ CUP CONFECTIONERS' SUGAR

1 In small bowl, stir together flour, cocoa, baking soda, baking powder, and salt.

2 In large bowl, with mixer at medium speed, beat butter, granulated sugar, and corn syrup until combined. Reduce speed to low and beat in chocolate, eggs, and vanilla until well blended. Beat in flour mixture until combined, scraping bowl occasionally with rubber spatula. Cover dough and refrigerate 1 hour.

3 Preheat oven to 350°F. Place confectioners' sugar in small bowl. Shape dough into 1-inch balls; roll in confectioners' sugar.

4 Place cookies, 1 inch apart, on ungreased large cookie sheet. Bake until set, about 8 minutes. With wide metal spatula, transfer cookies to wire rack to cool completely.

5 Repeat with remaining dough and confectioners' sugar.

EACH COOKIE: ABOUT 35 CALORIES | 1G PROTEIN | 6G CARBOHYDRATE | 1G TOTAL FAT (1G SATURATED) | 0.5G FIBER | 7MG CHOLESTEROL | 35MG SODIUM

CHOCOLATE-COCONUT BITES

Chocolate lovers will come running as soon as they smell these coconut-studded cookies baking in the oven. Fortunately, the bite-size morsels are ready to eat as soon as they are cool enough to hold.

ACTIVE TIME: 30 MINUTES PLUS CHILLING · **BAKE TIME:** 12 MINUTES PER BATCH
MAKES: 48 COOKIES

8 SQUARES (8 OUNCES) SEMISWEET CHOCOLATE, CHOPPED	¾ CUP SUGAR
6 TABLESPOONS BUTTER OR MARGARINE, CUT INTO PIECES	2 TEASPOONS VANILLA EXTRACT
⅓ CUP ALL-PURPOSE FLOUR	2 LARGE EGGS
¼ CUP UNSWEETENED COCOA	1 PACKAGE (6 OUNCES) SEMISWEET CHOCOLATE CHIPS (1 CUP)
½ TEASPOON BAKING POWDER	1 CUP FLAKED SWEETENED COCONUT
¼ TEASPOON SALT	

1 In 1-quart saucepan, melt chopped chocolate and butter over low heat, stirring occasionally, until smooth. Pour melted chocolate mixture into large bowl; cool to lukewarm, about 10 minutes.

2 Meanwhile, in small bowl, combine flour, cocoa, baking powder, and salt.

3 Stir sugar and vanilla into chocolate mixture until blended. Mix in eggs, one at a time. Add flour mixture, chocolate chips, and coconut and stir until combined. Cover with plastic wrap and refrigerate 1 hour.

4 Preheat oven to 350°F. Shape dough into 1½-inch balls. Place balls, 2 inches apart, on ungreased large cookie sheet.

5 Bake until set, 12 to 14 minutes. Cool on cookie sheet on wire rack 2 minutes. With wide metal spatula, carefully transfer cookies to wire rack to cool further. Clean edge of spatula after each batch, if necessary, for easier removal of cookies from cookie sheet.

6 Repeat with remaining dough.

EACH COOKIE: ABOUT 85 CALORIES | 1G PROTEIN | 10G CARBOHYDRATE | 5G TOTAL FAT (3G SATURATED) | 1G FIBER | 13MG CHOLESTEROL | 40MG SODIUM

CHOCOLATE SAMBUCA COOKIES

This seriously chocolate cookie, spiked with sambuca liqueur, makes an elegant after-dinner confection.

ACTIVE TIME: 30 MINUTES PLUS CHILLING · **BAKE TIME:** 10 MINUTES PER BATCH
MAKES: 48 COOKIES

---

12 SQUARES (12 OUNCES) SEMISWEET CHOCOLATE, CHOPPED

4 TABLESPOONS BUTTER OR MARGARINE

3 LARGE EGGS

⅓ CUP SAMBUCA (ANISE-FLAVORED LIQUEUR)

1 CUP GRANULATED SUGAR

1 CUP BLANCHED ALMONDS (4 OUNCES), FINELY GROUND

⅔ CUP ALL-PURPOSE FLOUR

¾ TEASPOON BAKING SODA

⅓ CUP CONFECTIONERS' SUGAR

1 In 2-quart saucepan, melt chocolate and butter over low heat, stirring frequently, until smooth. Remove saucepan from heat; cool chocolate mixture slightly.

2 In medium bowl, with wire whisk, mix eggs, sambuca, and ½ cup granulated sugar; blend in chocolate mixture.

3 With spoon, stir ground almonds, flour, and baking soda into chocolate mixture until combined (dough will be very soft). Cover bowl with plastic wrap and refrigerate at least 4 hours or overnight.

4 Preheat oven to 350°F. In small bowl, combine confectioners' sugar and remaining ½ cup granulated sugar. With lightly floured hands, roll dough by rounded tablespoons into balls. Roll balls in sugar mixture to coat. Place balls, about 2 inches apart, on ungreased large cookie sheet.

5 Bake until cookies are just set and look puffed and cracked, 10 to 12 minutes. Cool on cookie sheet on wire rack 1 minute. With wide metal spatula, transfer cookies to wire rack to cool completely.

6 Repeat with remaining dough and sugar mixture.

EACH COOKIE: ABOUT 85 CALORIES | 2G PROTEIN | 12G CARBOHYDRATE | 4G TOTAL FAT (0G SATURATED) | 1G FIBER | 13MG CHOLESTEROL | 20MG SODIUM

MEXICAN WEDDING COOKIES

Often called snowballs in America, these sugar-coated balls can also be made with almonds, walnuts, or toasted hazelnuts. In Mexico, where they originated, their name is *pastelitas de boda*. It is important to roll them in confectioners' sugar twice, once while they are still slightly warm and again after they have cooled or immediately before serving.

ACTIVE TIME: 25 MINUTES · **BAKE TIME:** 20 MINUTES PER BATCH
MAKES: 48 COOKIES

---

1 CUP PECANS (4 OUNCES)

1¾ CUPS CONFECTIONERS' SUGAR

1 CUP BUTTER (2 STICKS), CUT INTO 16 PIECES AND SOFTENED (DO NOT USE MARGARINE)

1 TEASPOON VANILLA EXTRACT

2 CUPS ALL-PURPOSE FLOUR

1 Preheat oven to 325°F.

2 In food processor with knife blade attached, process pecans and ¼ cup sugar until nuts are finely chopped. Add butter and vanilla and process until smooth, scraping down sides of processor with rubber spatula. Add flour and process until dough is combined and holds together.

3 With floured hands, shape dough by heaping tablespoons into 1-inch balls. Place balls 1½ inches apart on ungreased large cookie sheet. Bake until bottoms are lightly browned and cookies are very light golden brown, 20 to 22 minutes. With wide metal spatula, transfer to wire rack to cool.

4 Place remaining 1½ cups confectioners' sugar in pie plate. While cookies are still warm, roll in sugar until coated and place on wire rack to cool completely. When cool, reroll cookies in sugar until thoroughly coated.

5 Repeat with remaining dough and confectioners' sugar.

EACH COOKIE: ABOUT 85 CALORIES | 1G PROTEIN | 9G CARBOHYDRATE | 5G TOTAL FAT (3G SATURATED) | 0.5G FIBER | 10MG CHOLESTEROL | 40MG SODIUM

HONEY COOKIES

These mildly honey-sweetened and slightly salty cookies hail from Czechoslovakia.

ACTIVE TIME: 40 MINUTES PLUS CHILLING · **BAKE TIME:** 18 MINUTES PER BATCH
MAKES: 42 COOKIES

1 CUP BUTTER OR MARGARINE (2 STICKS), SOFTENED	2 CUPS ALL-PURPOSE FLOUR
¼ CUP HONEY	2 CUPS WALNUTS (8 OUNCES), CHOPPED
2 TEASPOONS VANILLA EXTRACT	½ TEASPOON SALT

1 In large bowl, with mixer at high speed, beat butter until creamy. Add honey and vanilla; beat until well blended. Reduce speed to low; beat in flour, walnuts, and salt until dough forms. Cover bowl with plastic wrap and refrigerate dough at least 1 hour.

2 Preheat oven to 325°F. With lightly floured hands, shape dough by heaping tablespoons into 1-inch balls. Place balls, about 2 inches apart, on ungreased large cookie sheet. Press floured four-tine fork across top of each ball.

3 Bake until golden, 18 to 22 minutes. With wide metal spatula, transfer cookies to wire rack to cool.

4 Repeat with remaining dough.

EACH COOKIE: ABOUT 105 CALORIES | 1G PROTEIN | 7G CARBOHYDRATE | 8G TOTAL FAT (1G SATURATED) | 0.5G FIBER | 0MG CHOLESTEROL | 85MG SODIUM

PRETZEL COOKIES

With their golden-brown glaze and a sprinkling of coarse decorating sugar, these pretty cookies look like salted pretzels. But one citrus-flavored bite reveals a scrumptious cookie.

ACTIVE TIME: 20 MINUTES · **BAKE TIME:** 25 MINUTES
MAKES: 18 COOKIES

½ CUP BUTTER OR MARGARINE (1 STICK), SOFTENED

⅓ CUP GRANULATED SUGAR

1 TEASPOON FRESHLY GRATED LEMON OR ORANGE PEEL

¼ TEASPOON SALT

1 LARGE EGG

2 LARGE EGG YOLKS

2 CUPS ALL-PURPOSE FLOUR

½ TEASPOON WATER

COARSE OR GRANULATED SUGAR FOR SPRINKLING

2 SQUARES (2 OUNCES) SEMISWEET CHOCOLATE, MELTED (OPTIONAL)

1 Preheat oven to 350°F.

2 In large bowl, with mixer at medium speed, beat butter and granulated sugar until creamy. Add lemon or orange peel, salt, egg, and 1 egg yolk; beat until well blended. Reduce speed to low; add flour and beat until combined.

3 Gather dough into ball and knead on lightly floured surface. With hands, divide dough into 20 pieces. Roll each piece into 11-inch-long rope. To shape each rope into a pretzel, form dough into an open loop then cross the ends and rest each one on bottom of loop. Place pretzels, 1 inch apart, on large ungreased cookie sheet.

4 In small cup, with fork, beat remaining egg yolk with water. Brush pretzels with glaze; sprinkle with coarse sugar. Bake until golden brown, 25 to 28 minutes. Cool on cookie sheet on wire rack 3 minutes. With wide metal spatula, transfer cookies to wire rack to cool completely. When cool, drizzle melted chocolate over cookies, if you like; let chocolate set before serving.

EACH COOKIE WITHOUT CHOCOLATE: ABOUT 115 CALORIES | 2G PROTEIN | 15G CARBOHYDRATE | 6G TOTAL FAT (4G SATURATED) | 0.5G FIBER | 44MG CHOLESTEROL | 80MG SODIUM

SUGAR TWISTS

Children will love to help shape these sparkly cookies. For variety, you can use different-colored sugars or a drizzle of melted white chocolate in place of the white sugar crystals.

ACTIVE TIME: 1 HOUR PLUS CHILLING · **BAKE TIME:** 11 MINUTES PER BATCH
MAKES: 120 COOKIES

1⅓ CUPS ALL-PURPOSE FLOUR

½ TEASPOON BAKING SODA

½ TEASPOON SALT

4 LARGE EGGS

1½ CUPS GRANULATED SUGAR

1 CUP BUTTER (2 STICKS), SOFTENED (DO NOT USE MARGARINE)

2 TEASPOONS VANILLA EXTRACT

WHITE SUGAR CRYSTALS

1 In small bowl, combine flour, baking soda, and salt. Separate 2 eggs, placing yolks in one small bowl and whites in another. Cover and reserve whites in refrigerator for brushing on cookies later.

2 In large bowl, with mixer at medium speed, beat granulated sugar and butter until creamy, occasionally scraping bowl with rubber spatula. Beat in whole eggs, egg yolks, and vanilla. Reduce speed to low; gradually beat in flour mixture until blended.

3 Divide dough into 4 equal pieces. Wrap each piece in plastic wrap and refrigerate until dough is firm enough to roll, at least 2 hours. (Or place dough in freezer for 30 minutes.)

4 Preheat oven to 350°F. Grease large cookie sheet.

5 On lightly floured surface with floured hands, press 1 piece of dough into 6" by 3" by ¾" rectangle; keep remaining dough refrigerated. Cut rectangle into 30 equal pieces. Roll each piece into a 6-inch-long rope. Transfer 1 rope at a time to prepared cookie sheet; gently shape into a loop, with ends over-lapping. Repeat with remaining ropes, placing cookies 1 inch apart. Brush cookies with reserved egg whites; sprinkle with sugar crystals.

6 Bake until lightly browned, 11 to 12 minutes. With wide metal spatula, transfer cookies to wire rack to cool.

7 Repeat with remaining dough, egg whites, and sugar crystals.

EACH COOKIE: ABOUT 40 CALORIES | 1G PROTEIN | 5G CARBOHYDRATE | 2G TOTAL FAT (1G SATURATED) | 0G FIBER | 12MG CHOLESTEROL | 36MG SODIUM

GARDEN-PARTY SUGAR COOKIES

Fresh thyme, lemon peel, and crystallized ginger bring complex flavor to these easy-to-make cookies. They're perfect with iced tea or lemonade.

ACTIVE TIME: 30 MINUTES PLUS CHILLING · **BAKE TIME:** 12 MINUTES PER BATCH
MAKES: 96 COOKIES

2½ CUPS ALL-PURPOSE FLOUR

1 TEASPOON BAKING SODA

1 TEASPOON CREAM OF TARTAR

½ TEASPOON SALT

1 CUP BUTTER OR MARGARINE (2 STICKS), SOFTENED

2 CUPS CONFECTIONERS' SUGAR

1 LARGE EGG

1 TABLESPOON FRESHLY GRATED LEMON PEEL

1 TABLESPOON FRESH THYME LEAVES (PREFERABLY LEMON THYME), MINCED

1 TABLESPOON MINCED CRYSTALLIZED GINGER

1 In medium bowl, combine flour, baking soda, cream of tartar, and salt.

2 In large bowl, with mixer at low speed, beat butter and confectioners' sugar until blended. Increase speed to high; beat until creamy. Reduce speed to low; beat in egg, lemon peel, thyme, and ginger. Beat in flour mixture just until blended.

3 Divide dough in half. Shape each half into 12" by 1½" squared-off log; wrap each log in plastic. Freeze until firm enough to slice, 2 hours. (Logs can be frozen up to 1 month.)

4 Preheat oven to 350°F. Cut 1 log crosswise into ¼-inch-thick slices. Place slices, 1 inch apart, on ungreased large cookie sheet. Bake until edges are golden brown, 12 to 14 minutes. With wide metal spatula, transfer to wire rack to cool.

5 Repeat with remaining dough.

EACH COOKIE: ABOUT 40 CALORIES | 0G PROTEIN | 5G CARBOHYDRATE | 2G TOTAL FAT (0G SATURATED) | 0G FIBER | 2MG CHOLESTEROL | 50MG SODIUM

ALMOND MACAROON FINGERS

It's hard to believe that cookies as chewy and rich as our chocolate-brushed macaroons are also low in fat, but it's the truth. For photo, see page 78.

ACTIVE TIME: 1 HOUR 30 MINUTES · **BAKE TIME:** 17 MINUTES PER BATCH
MAKES: 42 COOKIES

---

1   CAN (7 TO 8 OUNCES) ALMOND PASTE
½   CUP CONFECTIONERS' SUGAR
2   LARGE EGG WHITES
½   TEASPOON VANILLA EXTRACT

2   OUNCES (2 SQUARES) BITTERSWEET OR SEMISWEET CHOCOLATE, BROKEN INTO PIECES

1   Preheat oven to 300°F. Line 2 cookie sheets with parchment.

2   In food processor with knife blade attached, process almond paste and sugar until combined (a few small lumps will remain). Add whites and vanilla; pulse until well combined.

3   Spoon batter into decorating bag fitted with ½-inch star tip. Pipe batter into 3-inch-long fingers, 1 inch apart, onto prepared cookie sheets.

4   Bake macaroons until edges start to turn golden brown, 17 to 19 minutes, rotating sheets between racks halfway through baking. Cool on cookie sheets on wire racks. Repeat with remaining batter.

5   In microwave-safe cup, heat chocolate in microwave oven on High until soft and shiny, 1 minute. Remove from oven; stir until smooth. With pastry brush, brush chocolate on half of each macaroon; let set. Or refrigerate 5 minutes to set chocolate. Peel cookies from parchment.

EACH COOKIE: ABOUT 30 CALORIES | 1G PROTEIN | 5G CARBOHYDRATE | 1G TOTAL FAT (0G SATURATED) | 0.5G FIBER | 18MG CHOLESTEROL | 11MG SODIUM

LADYFINGERS

Homemade ladyfingers are so delicious that it is hard to believe they are so easy to make. You can serve them alone or use them to create old-fashioned desserts such as trifle.

ACTIVE TIME: 25 MINUTES · **BAKE TIME:** 10 MINUTES
MAKES: 48 LADYFINGERS

4 LARGE EGGS, SEPARATED	1 TEASPOON VANILLA EXTRACT
⅛ TEASPOON SALT	¾ CUP ALL-PURPOSE FLOUR
¾ CUP GRANULATED SUGAR	CONFECTIONERS' SUGAR

1 Preheat oven to 350°F. Grease and flour two large cookie sheets.

2 In small bowl, with mixer at high speed, beat egg whites and salt until soft peaks form when beaters are lifted. Beating at high speed, gradually sprinkle in ¼ cup granulated sugar, 1 tablespoon at a time, beating until sugar has dissolved and whites stand in stiff, glossy peaks when beaters are lifted.

3 In large bowl, with same beaters and with mixer at medium speed, beat egg yolks, remaining ½ cup granulated sugar, and vanilla until very thick and lemon-colored. With rubber spatula, fold in one-third of flour, then gently fold in remaining flour just until blended. Gently fold one-third of beaten egg whites into egg-yolk mixture. Fold in remaining egg whites just until blended.

4 Spoon half of batter into large pastry bag fitted with ½-inch plain tip. Pipe batter into 3-inch lengths, 1 inch apart, on prepared cookie sheets. If you like, with moistened finger, smooth edges. Lightly dust ladyfingers with confectioners' sugar. Repeat with remaining batter.

5 Bake until golden brown, 10 to 13 minutes, rotating cookie sheets between upper and lower oven racks halfway through baking. With wide metal spatula, transfer ladyfingers to wire racks to cool completely.

EACH COOKIE: ABOUT 30 CALORIES | 1G PROTEIN | 5G CARBOHYDRATE | 1G TOTAL FAT (0G SATURATED) | 0G FIBER | 18MG CHOLESTEROL | 11MG SODIUM

MERINGUE FINGERS

So much satisfaction for so few calories! The long, slow baking time at low temperature is essential to crisp the centers of the cookies without browning the outside.

ACTIVE TIME: 25 MINUTES PLUS COOLING · **BAKE TIME:** 1 HOUR PER BATCH
MAKES: 48 COOKIES

3	LARGE EGG WHITES	1	TEASPOON VANILLA EXTRACT
¼	TEASPOON CREAM OF TARTAR	2	SQUARES (2 OUNCES) SEMISWEET CHOCOLATE
⅛	TEASPOON SALT	1	TEASPOON VEGETABLE SHORTENING
½	CUP SUGAR		

1 Preheat oven to 200°F. Line two large cookie sheets with foil.

2 In medium bowl, with mixer at high speed, beat egg whites, cream of tartar, and salt until soft peaks form when beaters are lifted. Increase speed to high and gradually sprinkle in sugar, 2 tablespoons at a time, beating until sugar has dissolved. Add vanilla; continue beating until meringue stands in stiff, glossy peaks when beaters are lifted.

3 Spoon meringue into pastry bag fitted with ½-inch star tip. Pipe 3" by ½" fingers of meringue, about 1 inch apart, onto prepared cookie sheets.

4 Bake until set, 1 hour, rotating sheets between upper and lower oven racks halfway through baking. Cool on cookie sheets on wire racks, 10 minutes. With small metal spatula, transfer cookies to wire racks to cool completely.

5 When cookies have cooled, in small saucepan, heat chocolate and shortening over low heat, stirring occasionally, until melted and smooth. Remove saucepan from heat. Dip one end of each cookie into melted chocolate mixture; let dry on wire racks over sheet of waxed paper.

EACH COOKIE: ABOUT 15 CALORIES | 0G PROTEIN | 3G CARBOHYDRATE | 0G TOTAL FAT (0G SATURATED) | 0G FIBER | 0MG CHOLESTEROL | 10MG SODIUM

MADELEINES

The classic, shell-shaped, French sponge cakes extolled by Marcel Proust require a special pan for molding. But they taste so good a madeleine pan is worth the investment. It makes a nice butter and candy mold as well.

ACTIVE TIME: 25 MINUTES · **BAKE TIME:** 10 MINUTES PER BATCH
MAKES: 24 MADELEINES

1 CUP ALL-PURPOSE FLOUR	¾ CUP SUGAR
½ TEASPOON BAKING POWDER	3 LARGE EGGS
10 TABLESPOONS BUTTER (1¼ STICKS), SOFTENED (DO NOT USE MARGARINE)	1 LARGE EGG YOLK
	1½ TEASPOONS VANILLA EXTRACT

1 Preheat oven to 400°F. Generously grease and flour madeleine pan. In small bowl, combine flour and baking powder.

2 In large bowl, with mixer at medium speed, beat butter and sugar until creamy, about 2 minutes. Add eggs, egg yolk, and vanilla. Increase speed to high and beat until pale yellow, about 3 minutes. Reduce speed to low and beat in flour mixture just until blended, scraping bowl with rubber spatula.

3 Spoon batter by rounded tablespoons into prepared pan. Bake until edges are browned and tops spring back when lightly pressed, 10 to 12 minutes. Let madeleines cool in pan 1 minute. With tip of table knife, if needed, release madeleines onto wire rack to cool completely.

4 Wash, grease, and flour pan. Repeat with remaining batter.

EACH COOKIE: ABOUT 105 CALORIES | 2G PROTEIN | 11G CARBOHYDRATE | 6G TOTAL FAT (3G SATURATED) | 0G FIBER | 48MG CHOLESTEROL | 65MG SODIUM

NOISETTINES

Noisette means "hazelnut" in French. These delectable little hazelnut cookies re-create the flavor of "noisettine" tarts, a French bakery favorite.

ACTIVE TIME: 1 HOUR PLUS CHILLING · **BAKE TIME:** 30 MINUTES
MAKES: 24 COOKIES

1   SMALL PACKAGE (3 OUNCES) CREAM CHEESE, SOFTENED

½   CUP (1 STICK) PLUS 1 TABLESPOON BUTTER OR MARGARINE, SOFTENED

1   CUP ALL-PURPOSE FLOUR

1⅓   CUPS HAZELNUTS (FILBERTS, ABOUT 5.5 OUNCES)

⅔   CUP PACKED LIGHT BROWN SUGAR

1   LARGE EGG

1   TEASPOON VANILLA EXTRACT

1   In large bowl, with mixer at high speed, beat cream cheese and ½ cup butter until creamy. Reduce speed to low; add flour and beat until well mixed. Cover bowl with plastic wrap and refrigerate 30 minutes.

2   Meanwhile, preheat oven to 350°F. Toast and skin hazelnuts (see page 75).

3   Reserve 24 hazelnuts for garnish. In food processor with knife blade attached, process remaining hazelnuts and brown sugar until hazelnuts are finely ground.

4   Prepare filling: In medium bowl, with spoon, combine hazelnut mixture, egg, vanilla, and remaining 1 tablespoon butter.

5   With floured hands, divide chilled dough into 24 equal pieces (dough will be very soft). Gently press dough evenly onto bottom and up sides of twenty-four 1¾" by 1" ungreased miniature muffin-pan cups. Spoon filling by heaping teaspoons into each pastry cup; place 1 whole hazelnut on top of filling in each cup.

6   Bake until filling is set and crust is golden, 30 minutes. With tip of knife, loosen cookies from muffin-pan cups and place on wire rack to cool completely.

EACH COOKIE: ABOUT 135 CALORIES | 2G PROTEIN | 11G CARBOHYDRATE | 10G TOTAL FAT (2G SATURATED) | 1G FIBER | 13MG CHOLESTEROL | 75MG SODIUM

ANISETTE COOKIES

Both the dough and the glaze of these old-fashioned Italian cookie are flavored with anisette.

ACTIVE TIME: 1 HOUR PLUS CHILLING AND COOLING · **BAKE TIME:** 12 MINUTES PER BATCH
MAKES: 36 COOKIES

½ CUP BUTTER OR MARGARINE (1 STICK), SOFTENED

½ CUP GRANULATED SUGAR

3 LARGE EGGS

1 TEASPOON VANILLA EXTRACT

2 TEASPOONS ANISETTE (ANISE-FLAVORED LIQUEUR) OR ANISE EXTRACT

2½ CUPS ALL-PURPOSE FLOUR

1 TABLESPOON BAKING POWDER

¾ CUP CONFECTIONERS' SUGAR

2 TABLESPOONS WATER

RED AND GREEN SPRINKLES (OPTIONAL)

1 In large bowl, with mixer at low speed, beat butter and granulated sugar until blended. Increase speed to high; beat until creamy. At medium speed, beat in eggs, vanilla, and 1 teaspoon anisette, constantly scraping bowl with rubber spatula. Reduce speed to low; beat in flour and baking powder, occasionally scraping bowl. Shape dough into 4 balls. Wrap each ball in plastic and freeze at least 1 hour or refrigerate overnight.

2 Preheat oven to 350°F. On lightly floured surface, divide 1 ball of dough into 9 equal pieces; keep remaining dough refrigerated. With lightly floured hands, roll each piece of dough into a 7-inch-long rope; gently twist several times. Bring ends of rope together and pinch to seal.

3 Place cookies, about 2 inches apart, on ungreased large cookie sheet. Bake until bottoms are lightly browned, 12 minutes. With wide metal spatula, transfer cookies to wire rack to cool. Repeat with remaining dough.

4 When cookies are cool, prepare glaze: In small bowl, mix confectioners' sugar, remaining 1 teaspoon anisette, and water. With pastry brush, brush tops of cookies with glaze; place on rack. Top with sprinkles, if you like. Set cookies aside to allow glaze to dry, about 1 hour.

EACH COOKIE WITHOUT SPRINKLES: ABOUT 80 CALORIES | 1G PROTEIN | 12G CARBOHYDRATE | 3G TOTAL FAT (1G SATURATED) | 0G FIBER | 18MG CHOLESTEROL | 70MG SODIUM

SICILIAN SESAME COOKIES

Here are cookies you can serve as a snack any time of day, even early morning, because they're not too sweet. To coat the dough quickly, put the toasted sesame seeds in a small plastic bag, add the logs of dough one at a time, and shake gently.

ACTIVE TIME: 30 MINUTES · **BAKE TIME:** 30 MINUTES PER BATCH
MAKES: 48 COOKIES

1   CUP SESAME SEEDS (5 OUNCES)

2¼ CUPS ALL-PURPOSE FLOUR

¾   CUP SUGAR

2   TEASPOONS BAKING POWDER

¼   TEASPOON SALT

3   LARGE EGGS, BEATEN

4   TABLESPOONS BUTTER OR MARGARINE, MELTED

1   TEASPOON VANILLA EXTRACT

1   Preheat oven to 350°F. Spread sesame seeds in single layer on jelly-roll pan; bake, stirring once, until golden, 8 to 10 minutes. Cool on wire rack, then transfer to small bowl.

2   In large bowl, stir together flour, sugar, baking powder, and salt. In small bowl, stir together eggs, melted butter, and vanilla. Add egg mixture to flour mixture, stirring just until blended.

3   Transfer dough to lightly floured surface. With hands, knead dough five or six times until smooth. Divide dough into quarters. Roll 1 piece into a 24-inch-long rope; with knife, cut crosswise into twelve 2-inch logs.

4   Fill small bowl with water. Dip each log in the water and roll in the toasted sesame seeds until completely coated. Place logs, 1 inch apart, on two ungreased large cookie sheets. Bake until golden brown, 30 to 35 minutes, rotating sheets between upper and lower racks halfway through baking. With wide metal spatula, carefully transfer cookies to wire racks to cool completely. (Cookies will be soft at first but firm up as they cool.)

5   Repeat with remaining dough and sesame seeds.

EACH COOKIE: ABOUT 65 CALORIES | 2G PROTEIN | 9G CARBOHYDRATE | 3G TOTAL FAT (1G SATURATED) | 0.5G FIBER | 16MG CHOLESTEROL | 45MG SODIUM

ALMOND LEAVES

To make these lovely cookies in the traditional leaf shape, you will need a stencil spatula that has a leaf-shaped cutout in the center. However, they taste just as delicious if you drop teaspoons of batter on cool buttered trays and spread it into rounds or free-form shapes.

ACTIVE TIME: 65 MINUTES · **BAKE TIME:** 7 MINUTES PER BATCH
MAKES: 36 COOKIES

⅓ CUP ALMOND PASTE (3½ OUNCES), CRUMBLED

¼ CUP SUGAR

3 TABLESPOONS BUTTER OR MARGARINE, SOFTENED

1 LARGE EGG, SLIGHTLY BEATEN

¼ TEASPOON ALMOND EXTRACT

⅓ CUP PLUS 2 TABLESPOONS ALL-PURPOSE FLOUR

1 Preheat oven to 350°F. In small bowl, with mixer at medium speed, beat almond paste until softened. Add sugar and beat until smooth (a few small lumps will remain). Add butter and beat until well blended. Reduce speed to low and beat in egg and almond extract until incorporated. Stir in flour until just combined, scraping bowl occasionally with rubber spatula.
2 Generously butter two large cookie sheets. Spread batter by teaspoonfuls through leaf stencil spatula on prepared cookie sheets and smooth ⅛ inch thick with small wet metal spatula. Repeat with some of remaining batter, leaving 2 inches between leaves.
3 Bake until edges are golden, 7 to 9 minutes, rotating sheets between upper and lower racks halfway through baking. With wide metal spatula, transfer cookies to wire rack to cool completely.
4 Repeat with remaining batter.

EACH COOKIE: ABOUT 35 CALORIES | 1G PROTEIN | 4G CARBOHYDRATE | 2G TOTAL FAT (1G SATURATED) | 0G FIBER | 9MG CHOLESTEROL | 15MG SODIUM

CHOCOLATE ALMOND LEAVES

Prepare as above; cool. Melt **3½ squares (3½ ounces) semisweet chocolate.** Spread chocolate in thin layer over cooled cookies, marking veins of leaves with edge of small metal spatula. Let stand on wire racks until chocolate has set.

EACH COOKIE: ABOUT 50 CALORIES | 1G PROTEIN | 6G CARBOHYDRATE | 3G TOTAL FAT (1G SATURATED) | 0G FIBER | 9MG CHOLESTEROL | 15MG SODIUM

PIGNOLI COOKIES

Thanks to the food processor—and prepared almond paste—making these pine nut–topped Italian cookies is a breeze. We use a pastry bag to form the rounds to keep our fingers from getting sticky.

ACTIVE TIME: 25 MINUTES · **BAKE TIME:** 10 MINUTES PER BATCH
MAKES: 24 COOKIES

---

1 TUBE OR CAN (7 TO 8 OUNCES) ALMOND PASTE

¾ CUP CONFECTIONERS' SUGAR

1 LARGE EGG WHITE

1 TABLESPOON PLUS 1 TEASPOON HONEY

½ CUP PINE NUTS (PIGNOLI, 3 OUNCES)

1 Preheat oven to 350°F. Line two large cookie sheets with cooking parchment.

2 Crumble almond paste into food processor with knife blade attached. Add sugar and process until paste has texture of fine meal; transfer to large bowl. Add egg white and honey. With mixer at low speed, beat until dough is blended. Increase speed to medium-high and beat until very smooth, 5 minutes.

3 Spoon batter into pastry bag fitted with ½-inch round tip. Pipe 1¼-inch rounds, 2 inches apart, onto prepared cookie sheets. Brush cookies lightly with water and cover completely with pine nuts, pressing gently to make nuts stick.

4 Bake until golden brown, 10 to 12 minutes, rotating sheets between upper and lower oven racks halfway through baking. Slide parchment paper onto wire racks and let cookies cool on parchment paper.

5 Repeat with remaining dough and pine nuts.

EACH COOKIE: ABOUT 75 CALORIES | 2G PROTEIN | 9G CARBOHYDRATE | 4G TOTAL FAT (0G SATURATED) | 0.5G FIBER | 0MG CHOLESTEROL | 5MG SODIUM

PINE-NUT TASSIES

Folks will love these scrumptious tarts made with a cream-cheese crust and a toasted pine-nut and brown-sugar filling. Serve them for dessert or tea.

ACTIVE TIME: 40 MINUTES PLUS CHILLING · **BAKE TIME:** 30 MINUTES
MAKES: 24 COOKIES

1 CUP PINE NUTS (PIGNOLI, 6 OUNCES)	1 CUP ALL-PURPOSE FLOUR
1 SMALL PACKAGE (3 OUNCES) CREAM CHEESE, SOFTENED	2 TABLESPOONS GRANULATED SUGAR
	⅔ CUP PACKED LIGHT BROWN SUGAR
½ CUP (1 STICK) PLUS 1 TABLESPOON BUTTER OR MARGARINE, SOFTENED	1 LARGE EGG
	1 TEASPOON VANILLA EXTRACT

1 Preheat oven to 350°F. Toast ¾ cup pine nuts (see page 75). Cool completely.

2 Meanwhile, in large bowl, with mixer at high speed, beat cream cheese and ½ cup butter until creamy. Reduce speed to low; add flour and granulated sugar and beat until well mixed. Cover bowl with plastic wrap; refrigerate 30 minutes.

3 Prepare filling: In food processor with knife blade attached, process toasted pine nuts and brown sugar until pine nuts are finely ground.

4 In medium bowl, with spoon, combine pine-nut mixture, egg, vanilla, and remaining 1 tablespoon butter.

5 With floured hands, divide chilled dough into 24 equal pieces (dough will be very soft). With floured fingertips, gently press dough evenly onto bottom and up sides of twenty-four 1¾" by 1" ungreased miniature muffin-pan cups. Spoon filling by heaping teaspoons into each pastry cup; sprinkle with remaining ¼ cup pine nuts.

6 Bake until filling is set and crust is golden, 30 minutes. With tip of knife, loosen cookie cups from muffin-pan cups and place on wire rack to cool completely.

EACH COOKIE: ABOUT 125 CALORIES | 2G PROTEIN | 12G CARBOHYDRATE | 8G TOTAL FAT (2G SATURATED) | 0.5G FIBER | 13MG CHOLESTEROL | 75MG SODIUM

ALMOND-ANISE BISCOTTI

The crispy low-fat Italian cookies called biscotti took America by storm in the late 1980s. Originally served with coffee or after-dinner liqueurs, they now appear in lunch boxes, cookie jars, and bake sales. Here, soaking the anise seeds in liqueur softens them and releases their delicious flavor.

ACTIVE TIME: 25 MINUTES PLUS COOLING · **BAKE TIME:** 55 MINUTES
MAKES: 120 COOKIES

1   TABLESPOON ANISE SEEDS, CRUSHED

1   TABLESPOON ANISE-FLAVORED APERITIF OR LIQUEUR

2   CUPS ALL-PURPOSE FLOUR

1   CUP SUGAR

1   CUP WHOLE ALMONDS (4 OUNCES), TOASTED (SEE PAGE 75) AND COARSELY CHOPPED

1   TEASPOON BAKING POWDER

⅛   TEASPOON SALT

3   LARGE EGGS

1   Preheat oven to 325°F. In medium bowl, combine anise seeds and anise-flavored aperitif; let stand 10 minutes.

2   Grease large cookie sheet. In large bowl, combine flour, sugar, chopped almonds, baking powder, and salt. With wire whisk, beat eggs into anise mixture. With wooden spoon, stir egg mixture into flour mixture until blended.

3   Divide dough in half. Drop each half by spoonfuls down length of prepared cookie sheet, creating 2 rows. With floured hands, flatten and shape each half into a 15-inch-long log, leaving about 3 inches between logs. (Dough will be sticky.) Bake until golden and toothpick inserted in center comes out clean, about 40 minutes. Cool on cookie sheet on wire rack, 10 minutes.

4   Transfer logs to cutting board. With serrated knife, cut each log crosswise on diagonal into ¼-inch-thick slices. Place slices, cut side down, on two ungreased cookie sheets. Bake 15 minutes, turning slices over once and rotating cookie sheets between upper and lower oven racks halfway through baking. With wide metal spatula, transfer biscotti to wire racks to cool completely. (Biscotti will harden as they cool.)

EACH COOKIE: ABOUT 25 CALORIES | 1G PROTEIN | 4G CARBOHYDRATE | 1G TOTAL FAT (0G SATURATED) | 0G FIBER | 6MG CHOLESTEROL | 8MG SODIUM

SHAPING BISCOTTI

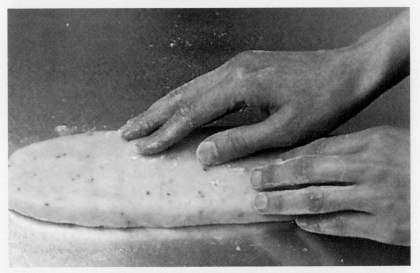

Step 1: Drop the dough by spoonfuls down the length of the cookie sheet. With lightly floured hands, flatten and shape it into a log of even thickness.

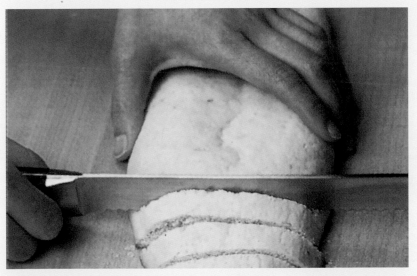

Step 2: After the first baking, slice the slightly cooled loaf with a serrated knife, using a gentle but confident sawing motion.

GINGER BISCOTTI

Small chunks of crystallized ginger give these crisp cookies a piquant bite. Be sure to cool them completely, then pack into a tight jar to keep them crisp.

ACTIVE TIME: 25 MINUTES PLUS COOLING · **BAKE TIME:** 50 MINUTES
MAKES: 48 COOKIES

3	CUPS ALL-PURPOSE FLOUR	½ CUP GRANULATED SUGAR
1	TABLESPOON GROUND GINGER	½ CUP PACKED LIGHT BROWN SUGAR
2	TEASPOONS BAKING POWDER	3 LARGE EGGS
¼	TEASPOON SALT	½ CUP FINELY CHOPPED CRYSTALLIZED GINGER
½	CUP BUTTER OR MARGARINE (1 STICK), SOFTENED	

1 Preheat oven to 350°F. Grease large cookie sheet. In medium bowl, stir together flour, ground ginger, baking powder, and salt.

2 In large bowl, with mixer at medium speed, beat butter and granulated and brown sugars until light and creamy. Beat in eggs, one at a time. Set speed to low and beat in flour mixture until combined; stir in crystallized ginger.

3 Divide dough in half. Drop each half by spoonfuls down length of pre-pared cookie sheet, creating 2 rows. With floured hands, flatten and shape each half into a 12-inch-long log, leaving about 3 inches between logs. Bake until toothpick inserted in center of logs comes out clean, about 30 minutes. Cool logs on cookie sheet on wire rack 10 minutes.

4 Transfer logs to cutting board. With serrated knife, cut each log cross-wise on diagonal into ½-inch-thick slices. Place slices, cut side down, on two ungreased cookie sheets. Bake until golden, 20 minutes, turning slices over and rotating sheets between upper and lower racks halfway through baking. With wide metal spatula, transfer biscotti to wire racks to cool completely. (Biscotti will harden as they cool.)

EACH COOKIE: ABOUT 90 CALORIES | 1G PROTEIN | 15G CARBOHYDRATE | 3G TOTAL FAT (2G SATURATED) | 0.5G FIBER | 21MG CHOLESTEROL | 65MG SODIUM

CHOCOLATE AND DRIED CHERRY BISCOTTI

For a tasty all-American twist, we added dried tart cherries to the original Italian twice-baked chocolate cookie.

ACTIVE TIME: 30 MINUTES PLUS COOLING · **BAKE TIME:** 45 MINUTES
MAKES: 48 COOKIES

---

1 TEASPOON INSTANT ESPRESSO-COFFEE POWDER	2 SQUARES (2 OUNCES) SEMISWEET CHOCOLATE, CHOPPED
1 TEASPOON HOT WATER	½ CUP BUTTER OR MARGARINE (1 STICK), SOFTENED
2½ CUPS ALL-PURPOSE FLOUR	1⅓ CUPS SUGAR
¾ CUP UNSWEETENED COCOA	3 LARGE EGGS
1 TABLESPOON BAKING POWDER	¾ CUP DRIED TART CHERRIES, COARSELY CHOPPED
½ TEASPOON SALT	

1 Preheat oven to 350°F. Grease and flour large cookie sheet. In cup, dissolve espresso powder in hot water; set aside.

2 In medium bowl, combine flour, cocoa, baking powder, and salt. In heavy 1-quart saucepan, melt chocolate over low heat, stirring frequently, until smooth. Remove pan from heat; cool.

3 In large bowl, with mixer at medium speed, beat butter and sugar until light and fluffy. Reduce speed to low; add eggs, one at a time, and beat until blended. Add cooled chocolate and espresso; beat until blended. Add flour mixture and beat just until blended. Knead in cherries by hand.

4 Divide dough in half. Drop by spoonfuls down length of ungreased cookie sheet, creating 2 rows. With floured hands, flatten and shape each half into a 12-inch-long log, leaving about 3 inches between logs. With pastry brush, brush off any excess flour. Bake until lightly browned, about 30 minutes. Cool on cookie sheet on wire rack 10 minutes.

5 Transfer loaves to cutting board. With serrated knife, cut each loaf crosswise on diagonal into ½-inch-thick slices. Place slices, cut side down, on same cookie sheet. Return to oven and bake 15 to 20 minutes to dry biscotti. With wide metal spatula, transfer biscotti to wire racks to cool completely. (Biscotti will harden as they cool.)

EACH COOKIE: ABOUT 85 CALORIES | 1G PROTEIN | 14G CARBOHYDRATE | 3G TOTAL FAT (2G SATURATED) | 1G FIBER | 17MG CHOLESTEROL | 79MG SODIUM

CHOCOLATE CHIP BISCOTTI

Mini chocolate chips and chopped toasted walnuts are a welcome addition to this otherwise traditional recipe.

ACTIVE TIME: 45 MINUTES PLUS COOLING · **BAKE TIME:** 40 MINUTES
MAKES: 60 COOKIES

---

2   CUPS ALL-PURPOSE FLOUR

1   CUP SUGAR

1   TEASPOON BAKING POWDER

¼   TEASPOON SALT

PINCH GROUND CINNAMON

4   TABLESPOONS COLD BUTTER OR MARGARINE, CUT INTO PIECES

3   LARGE EGGS, LIGHTLY BEATEN

1   PACKAGE (6 OUNCES) SEMISWEET CHOCOLATE MINI CHIPS (1 CUP)

1   CUP WALNUTS (4 OUNCES), TOASTED (SEE PAGE 75) AND COARSELY CHOPPED

1   TEASPOON VANILLA EXTRACT

1   Preheat oven to 350°F. In large bowl, mix flour, sugar, baking powder, salt, and cinnamon. With pastry blender or two knives used in scissor-fashion, cut in butter until mixture resembles fine crumbs.

2   Spoon 1 tablespoon beaten eggs into cup; reserve. Add chocolate chips, walnuts, vanilla, and remaining beaten eggs to flour mixture; stir until evenly moistened. Knead mixture a few times by hand in bowl until dough forms.

3   On floured surface, with floured hands, divide dough into quarters. Shape each quarter into a 9" by 2" log. Place logs crosswise, 4 inches apart, on two large ungreased cookie sheets. With pastry brush, brush tops and sides of logs with reserved egg. Bake until lightly browned, about 25 minutes. Cool logs on cookie sheet on wire rack 10 minutes.

4   Transfer 1 log to cutting board. With serrated knife, cut warm log crosswise on diagonal into ½-inch-thick slices. Place slices upright, ¼ inch apart, on same cookie sheets. Repeat with remaining logs. Return to oven and bake 15 minutes to dry biscotti, rotating sheets between upper and lower oven racks halfway through baking. Cool completely on cookie sheets on wire racks. (Biscotti will harden as they cool.)

EACH COOKIE: ABOUT 65 CALORIES | 1G PROTEIN | 9G CARBOHYDRATE | 3G TOTAL FAT (0G SATURATED) | 0.5G FIBER | 1MG CHOLESTEROL | 30MG SODIUM

CHOCOLATE-BROWNIE BISCOTTI

Enjoy rich brownie flavor, Italian style! These crisp chocolate cookies are a quick way to get your chocolate fix.

ACTIVE TIME: 45 MINUTES PLUS COOLING · **BAKE TIME:** 50 MINUTES
MAKES: 48 COOKIES

2½ CUPS ALL-PURPOSE FLOUR

1⅓ CUPS SUGAR

¾ CUP UNSWEETENED COCOA

2 TEASPOONS BAKING POWDER

½ TEASPOON BAKING SODA

½ TEASPOON SALT

½ CUP BUTTER OR MARGARINE (1 STICK), MELTED

3 LARGE EGGS

2 TEASPOONS VANILLA EXTRACT

1 CUP ALMONDS (4 OUNCES), TOASTED (SEE PAGE 75) AND COARSELY CHOPPED

4 SQUARES (4 OUNCES) SEMISWEET CHOCOLATE, COARSELY CHOPPED

1 Preheat oven to 325°F. In medium bowl, mix flour, sugar, cocoa, baking powder, baking soda, and salt.

2 In large bowl, with mixer at medium speed, beat butter, eggs, and vanilla until mixed. Reduce speed to low; gradually add flour mixture and beat just until blended. Knead in almonds and chocolate by hand until combined.

3 Divide dough in half. Drop by spoonfuls down length of ungreased cookie sheet, creating two rows. With floured hands, flatten and shape each half into a 12" by 3" log, leaving about 3 inches between logs. Bake until lightly browned, about 30 minutes. Cool on cookie sheet on wire rack 15 minutes.

4 Transfer logs to cutting board. With serrated knife, cut each log crosswise on diagonal into ½-inch-thick slices. Place slices upright, ¼ inch apart, on same cookie sheet. Return to oven and bake 20 minutes to dry biscotti. Cool completely on cookie sheet on wire rack. (Biscotti will harden as they cool.)

EACH COOKIE: ABOUT 100 CALORIES | 2G PROTEIN | 13G CARBOHYDRATE | 5G TOTAL FAT (2G SATURATED) | 2G FIBER | 19MG CHOLESTEROL | 79MG SODIUM

MANDELBROT

An Eastern European cookie, mandelbrot, or almond bread, is baked in logs, sliced, and rebaked just like biscotti. There are many variations on the classic recipe. Some feature nuts; others dried fruit, chocolate pieces, or a swirl of cocoa.

ACTIVE TIME: 30 MINUTES PLUS COOLING · **BAKE TIME:** 37 MINUTES
MAKES: 48 COOKIES

3¾ CUPS ALL-PURPOSE FLOUR

2 TEASPOONS BAKING POWDER

½ TEASPOON SALT

3 LARGE EGGS

1 CUP SUGAR

¾ CUP VEGETABLE OIL

2 TEASPOONS VANILLA EXTRACT

¼ TEASPOON ALMOND EXTRACT

1 TEASPOON FRESHLY GRATED ORANGE PEEL

1 CUP BLANCHED ALMONDS (4 OUNCES), COARSELY CHOPPED AND TOASTED (SEE PAGE 75) UNTIL GOLDEN

1   Preheat oven to 350°F. In large bowl, stir together flour, baking powder, and salt.

2   In separate large bowl, with mixer at medium speed, beat eggs and sugar until mixture is light lemon color. Add oil, vanilla and almond extracts, and orange peel and beat until blended. With wooden spoon, beat in flour mixture until combined. Stir in almonds.

3   Divide dough in half. Drop each half by spoonfuls down length of ungreased cookie sheet. With lightly floured hands, shape each half into 12-inch-long log, leaving 4 inches between logs (dough will be slightly sticky). Bake until lightly colored and firm, 30 minutes. Cool on cookie sheet on wire rack 10 minutes.

4   Transfer logs to cutting board. With serrated knife, cut each log crosswise into ½-inch-thick slices. Place slices, cut side down, on two ungreased cookie sheets. Bake until golden, 7 to 8 minutes, turning slices over and rotating sheets between upper and lower racks halfway through baking. With wide metal spatula, transfer cookies to wire racks to cool completely.

EACH COOKIE: ABOUT 105 CALORIES | 2G PROTEIN | 12G CARBOHYDRATE | 5G TOTAL FAT (1G SATURATED) | 0.5G FIBER | 13MG CHOLESTEROL | 50MG SODIUM

GREEK CINNAMON PAXIMADIA

Here's a Greek version of biscotti (*paximadia* is Greek for "biscuits") amply seasoned with cinnamon.

ACTIVE TIME: 1 HOUR PLUS COOLING · **BAKE TIME:** 50 MINUTES
MAKES: 64 COOKIES

½ CUP BUTTER OR MARGARINE (1 STICK), SOFTENED

½ CUP VEGETABLE SHORTENING

1½ CUPS SUGAR

3 LARGE EGGS

1 TEASPOON VANILLA EXTRACT

4 TO 4½ CUPS ALL-PURPOSE FLOUR

2 TEASPOONS BAKING POWDER

½ TEASPOON BAKING SODA

1½ TEASPOONS GROUND CINNAMON

1 In large bowl, with mixer at low speed, beat butter, shortening, and 1 cup sugar until blended. Increase speed to high; beat until light and fluffy, about 5 minutes. At low speed, add eggs, one at a time, and vanilla; beat until well mixed.

2 Gradually add 3 cups flour, baking powder, and baking soda; beat until well blended. With wooden spoon, stir in 1 cup flour until soft dough forms. If necessary, add additional flour (up to ½ cup) until dough is easy to handle.

3 Preheat oven to 350°F. Divide dough into 4 equal pieces. On lightly floured surface, shape each piece of dough into 8-inch-long log. Place 2 logs, about 4 inches apart, on each of two ungreased large cookie sheets. Flatten each log to 2½ inches wide.

4 Bake until lightly browned and toothpick inserted in center comes out clean, 20 minutes, rotating cookie sheets between upper and lower oven racks halfway through baking. (During baking, logs will spread and become loaves.) In pie plate, mix remaining ½ cup sugar and cinnamon.

5 Transfer hot loaves to cutting board. With serrated knife, cut crosswise on diagonal into ½-inch-thick slices. Coat slices with cinnamon-sugar. Return slices, cut side down, to same cookie sheets. Bake 15 minutes rotating cookie sheets between upper and lower racks halfway through. Turn slices over and return to oven; bake until golden, 15 minutes longer, again rotating cookie sheets between racks halfway through baking time. Transfer cookies to wire racks to cool.

EACH COOKIE: ABOUT 80 CALORIES | 1G PROTEIN | 1G CARBOHYDRATE | 4G TOTAL FAT (1G SATURATED) | 0.5G FIBER | 10MG CHOLESTEROL | 45MG SODIUM

CINNAMON SPIRALS

A spiral of aromatic spice runs through a cream-cheese dough. The result is a delicious contrast of colors and flavors.

ACTIVE TIME: 40 MINUTES PLUS CHILLING · **BAKE TIME:** 12 MINUTES PER BATCH

MAKES: 60 COOKIES

½ CUP BUTTER OR MARGARINE (1 STICK), SOFTENED

4 OUNCES CREAM CHEESE, SOFTENED

1¼ CUPS ALL-PURPOSE FLOUR

¼ TEASPOON SALT

⅓ CUP SUGAR

1 TEASPOON GROUND CINNAMON

1 In large bowl, with mixer at medium speed, beat butter and cream cheese until creamy, about 2 minutes. Reduce speed to low; gradually beat in flour and salt until well mixed, occasionally scraping bowl with rubber spatula.

2 On sheet of plastic wrap, pat dough into small rectangle. Wrap dough in plastic and refrigerate until dough is firm enough to roll, 1 hour. (Or freeze dough for 30 minutes.)

3 Meanwhile, in small bowl, mix sugar and cinnamon; set aside.

4 On lightly floured surface, with floured rolling pin, roll cookie dough into 15" by 12" rectangle. Sprinkle cinnamon-sugar mixture evenly over dough. Starting from one long side, tightly roll rectangle jelly-roll fashion. Brush last ½ inch of dough with water to help seal edge. Cut log crosswise in half. Slide logs onto ungreased cookie sheet; cover with plastic wrap and refrigerate until dough is firm enough to slice, 2 hours. (Or freeze dough for 45 minutes.)

5 Preheat oven to 400°F. Remove 1 log from refrigerator or freezer. With serrated knife, cut log crosswise into ¼-inch-thick slices. Place slices, ½ inch apart, on ungreased large cookie sheet. Bake until lightly browned, 12 to 14 minutes. With wide metal spatula, transfer cookies to wire rack to cool.

6 Repeat with remaining dough.

EACH COOKIE: ABOUT 35 CALORIES | 1G PROTEIN | 3G CARBOHYDRATE | 2G TOTAL FAT (2G SATURATED) | 0G FIBER | 6MG CHOLESTEROL | 32MG SODIUM

ALMOND SLICES

These crisp, thin cookies are a lovely teatime treat—so lovely that we've provided instructions for a huge batch. You'll be surprised how quickly they disappear, but if you want to freeze some of the dough for later use, just wrap it in heavy-duty aluminum foil, pack in an airtight container, and freeze for up to three months.

ACTIVE TIME: 45 MINUTES PLUS FREEZING · **BAKE TIME:** 15 MINUTES PER BATCH
MAKES: 256 COOKIES

1½ CUPS BUTTER (3 STICKS), MELTED (DO NOT USE MARGARINE)

1 CUP PACKED LIGHT BROWN SUGAR

1 CUP GRANULATED SUGAR

3 LARGE EGGS

1 TEASPOON VANILLA EXTRACT

½ TEASPOON LEMON EXTRACT

1 CUP SLIVERED BLANCHED ALMONDS (4 OUNCES), FINELY GROUND

5½ CUPS ALL-PURPOSE FLOUR

2 TEASPOONS GROUND CINNAMON

1½ TEASPOONS BAKING SODA

1 TEASPOON GROUND NUTMEG

1 TEASPOON SALT

1 In large bowl, with spoon, combine melted butter and brown and granulated sugars. Add eggs, vanilla and lemon extracts, and ground almonds; beat until well combined. Stir in flour, cinnamon, baking soda, nutmeg, and salt until dough forms. Cover bowl with plastic wrap and freeze dough until easy to handle, 1 hour.

2 Divide dough into 8 pieces. On lightly floured surface, with floured hands, shape each piece into 6-inch-long log. Wrap each log in waxed paper (see Step 1 photo, opposite) and freeze until firm enough to slice, at least 4 hours or overnight.

3 Preheat oven to 350°F. Grease two large cookie sheets. Slice 1 log into very thin (about 3⁄16-inch-thick) slices (see Step 2 photo, opposite). Keep remaining dough refrigerated. Place slices, 1½ inches apart, on prepared cookie sheets. Bake until browned, 15 minutes, rotating sheets between upper and lower oven racks halfway through baking. With wide metal spatula, transfer cookies to wire rack to cool.

4 Repeat with remaining dough.

EACH COOKIE: ABOUT 25 CALORIES | 0G PROTEIN | 3G CARBOHYDRATE | 1G TOTAL FAT (0G SATURATED) | 1G FIBER | 5MG CHOLESTEROL | 25MG SODIUM

SHAPING & SLICING ICEBOX COOKIES

Step 1: Shape the dough roughly into a log, then use the waxed paper to roll and smooth it into a cylinder of even thickness.

Step 2: As you slice the log of dough, turn it every few cuts so that the bottom doesn't become flattened.

ANISE SLICES

These aromatic cookies are perfect with a cup of tea or coffee. If you don't have a mortar and pestle to crush the anise seeds, you can coarsely grind them in a spice grinder. Or place them in a plastic bag and crush them with a rolling pin.

ACTIVE TIME: 30 MINUTES PLUS CHILLING · **BAKE TIME:** 12 MINUTES PER BATCH
MAKES: 88 COOKIES

½ CUP BUTTER (1 STICK), SOFTENED (DO NOT USE MARGARINE)

¾ CUP SUGAR

1 LARGE EGG

½ TEASPOON VANILLA EXTRACT

1¾ CUPS ALL-PURPOSE FLOUR

1 TABLESPOON ANISE SEEDS, CRUSHED

½ TEASPOON BAKING POWDER

¼ TEASPOON SALT

1 In large bowl, with mixer at medium speed, beat butter and sugar until creamy, about 1 minute, occasionally scraping bowl with rubber spatula. Reduce speed to low; beat in egg and vanilla until blended. Beat in flour, anise seeds, baking powder, and salt until well combined, occasionally scraping bowl.

2 Divide dough in half. Shape each half into 5½" by 2" rectangle. Wrap each rectangle in plastic wrap and refrigerate until dough is firm enough to slice, 2 hours. (Or freeze dough for 1 hour.)

3 Preheat oven to 350°F. Grease large cookie sheet. With knife, cut 1 rectangle crosswise into scant ⅛-inch-thick slices; keep remaining dough refrigerated. Place cookies, 1 inch apart, on prepared cookie sheet. Bake cookies until lightly browned, 12 to 14 minutes. With wide metal spatula, transfer cookies to wire rack to cool.

4 Repeat with remaining dough.

EACH COOKIE: ABOUT 25 CALORIES | 0G PROTEIN | 3G CARBOHYDRATE | 2G TOTAL FAT (1G SATURATED) | 1G FIBER | 6MG CHOLESTEROL | 21MG SODIUM

SPICY ALMOND SLICES

The spicy aroma of these almond cookies baking is so welcoming that family and guests will head for the kitchen to see what's for dessert.

ACTIVE TIME: 25 MINUTES PLUS CHILLING · **BAKE TIME:** 10 MINUTES PER BATCH
MAKES: 80 COOKIES

3½ CUPS ALL-PURPOSE FLOUR

1 TABLESPOON GROUND CINNAMON

1 TEASPOON BAKING SODA

½ TEASPOON GROUND CLOVES

½ TEASPOON GROUND NUTMEG

½ TEASPOON SALT

1 CUP BUTTER OR MARGARINE
(2 STICKS), SOFTENED

1 CUP GRANULATED SUGAR

¾ CUP PACKED DARK BROWN SUGAR

2 LARGE EGGS

1 TEASPOON VANILLA EXTRACT

2 CUPS SLICED BLANCHED ALMONDS
(8 OUNCES)

1 In medium bowl, combine flour, cinnamon, baking soda, cloves, nutmeg, and salt. In large bowl, with mixer at medium speed, beat butter and granulated and brown sugars until light and fluffy. Beat in eggs, one at a time; add vanilla. Reduce speed to low; beat in flour mixture just until blended. With wooden spoon, stir in almonds (dough will be stiff).
2 Divide dough in half. Shape each half into 10" by 3" by 1" rectangle; wrap each piece in plastic and refrigerate overnight, or freeze until very firm, at least 2 hours.
3 Preheat oven to 375°F. Cut 1 rectangle crosswise into ¼-inch-thick slices; keep remaining dough refrigerated. Place slices, 1 inch apart, on two ungreased cookie sheets. Bake until edges are browned, 10 to 12 minutes, rotating cookie sheets between upper and lower oven racks halfway through baking. With wide metal spatula, transfer cookies to wire racks to cool completely.
4 Repeat with remaining dough.

EACH COOKIE: ABOUT 80 CALORIES | 1G PROTEIN | 9G CARBOHYDRATE | 4G TOTAL FAT
(2G SATURATED) | 0.5G FIBER | 12MG CHOLESTEROL | 58MG SODIUM

LEMON SLICES

The silky, melt-in-your-mouth texture of these thinly sliced lemon cookies comes from confectioners' sugar. For a special treat, sandwich them with lemon frosting or bittersweet chocolate.

ACTIVE TIME: 30 MINUTES PLUS CHILLING · **BAKE TIME:** 12 MINUTES PER BATCH
MAKES: 48 COOKIES

---

2 CUPS ALL-PURPOSE FLOUR	½ CUP PLUS 2 TABLESPOONS GRANULATED SUGAR
¼ TEASPOON BAKING POWDER	½ CUP CONFECTIONERS' SUGAR
¼ TEASPOON SALT	½ TEASPOON VANILLA EXTRACT
2 TO 3 LARGE LEMONS	
¾ CUP BUTTER OR MARGARINE (1½ STICKS), SOFTENED	

1 In medium bowl, stir together flour, baking powder, and salt. From lemons, grate 1 tablespoon peel and squeeze 2 tablespoons juice.

2 In large bowl, with mixer at medium speed, beat butter, ½ cup granulated sugar, and confectioners' sugar until creamy. Beat in lemon peel and juice and vanilla until blended. Reduce speed to low and beat in flour mixture just until combined.

3 Divide dough in half. Shape each half into 6-inch-long log. Wrap each log in waxed paper (see photo, page 117) and refrigerate overnight. (If using margarine, freeze overnight.)

4 Preheat oven to 350°F. Cut 1 log crosswise into scant ¼-inch-thick slices; keep remaining log refrigerated. Place slices, 1½ inches apart, on ungreased large cookie sheet. Sprinkle slices lightly with some of remaining 2 tablespoons granulated sugar. Bake until edges are lightly browned, 12 minutes. Cool on cookie sheet on wire rack 2 minutes. With wide metal spatula, transfer to wire racks to cool completely.

5 Repeat with remaining dough and granulated sugar.

EACH COOKIE: ABOUT 35 CALORIES | 1G PROTEIN | 8G CARBOHYDRATE | 3G TOTAL FAT (1G SATURATED) | 0G FIBER | 8MG CHOLESTEROL | 44MG SODIUM

LEMON CORNMEAL THINS

Grated lemon peel contributes lots of piquant flavor. Similar to an Italian recipe called *zaleti*, these cookies are made with cornmeal, so they're nice and crunchy.

ACTIVE TIME: 30 MINUTES PLUS CHILLING · **BAKE TIME:** 16 MINUTES PER BATCH
MAKES: 56 COOKIES

¾ CUP BUTTER OR MARGARINE (1½ STICKS), SOFTENED

1 CUP SUGAR

2 LARGE EGGS

1 TABLESPOON FRESHLY GRATED LEMON PEEL

2 TEASPOONS VANILLA EXTRACT

1½ CUPS ALL-PURPOSE FLOUR

1½ CUPS YELLOW CORNMEAL

¾ TEASPOON BAKING POWDER

½ TEASPOON SALT

1 In large bowl, with mixer at medium speed, beat butter and sugar until creamy. Reduce speed to low and beat in eggs, lemon peel, and vanilla (mixture may look curdled). Gradually beat in flour, cornmeal, baking powder, and salt just until dough is evenly moistened.

2 With floured hands, divide dough in half. Shape each half into a 7" by 2" brick. Wrap each brick in plastic and refrigerate overnight, or freeze dough 1 hour. (If using margarine, freeze dough at least 6 hours.)

3 Preheat oven to 350°F. Grease large cookie sheet. With serrated knife, cut 1 brick crosswise into ¼-inch-thick slices. Place slices, 1 inch apart, on prepared cookie sheet. Bake until edges are golden, 16 to 18 minutes. With wide metal spatula, transfer cookies to wire rack to cool.

4 Repeat with remaining dough.

EACH COOKIE: ABOUT 70 CALORIES | 1G PROTEIN | 9G CARBOHYDRATE | 3G TOTAL FAT (2G SATURATED) | 0.5G FIBER | 15MG CHOLESTEROL | 55 MG SODIUM

COCONUT THINS

Flecks of toasted coconut make a pretty pattern on wafer-thin cookies. It is essential that the dough be very cold and firm, or it will be difficult to cut thinly.

ACTIVE TIME: 30 MINUTES PLUS CHILLING · **BAKE TIME:** 8 MINUTES PER BATCH
MAKES: 112 COOKIES

2 CUPS (6 OUNCES) FLAKED SWEETENED COCONUT	¾ CUP BUTTER OR MARGARINE (1½ STICKS), SOFTENED
1¾ CUPS ALL-PURPOSE FLOUR	1 CUP SUGAR
¼ CUP CORNSTARCH	1 LARGE EGG
½ TEASPOON BAKING POWDER	½ TEASPOON VANILLA EXTRACT
⅛ TEASPOON GROUND NUTMEG	¼ TEASPOON ALMOND EXTRACT
⅛ TEASPOON SALT	

1 Preheat oven to 350°F. In jelly-roll pan, toast coconut, stirring occasionally, until lightly golden, 9 to 10 minutes. In large bowl, stir together toasted coconut, flour, cornstarch, baking powder, nutmeg, and salt.

2 In separate large bowl, with mixer at medium speed, beat butter and sugar until light and fluffy. Beat in egg and vanilla and almond extracts. Reduce speed to low and beat in flour mixture until well combined.

3 Divide dough in half. On separate sheets of waxed paper, shape each half into 14" by 1½" log. Wrap each log in the waxed paper, rolling it up tightly (see photo, page 117). Refrigerate several hours, until very firm; or label, date, and freeze for up to 3 months.

4 Preheat oven to 350°F. Cut 1 log crosswise into ¼-inch-thick slices; keep remaining dough refrigerated. Place slices, 1 inch apart, on two ungreased large cookie sheets. Bake until edges are golden brown, 8 to 9 minutes, rotating sheets between upper and lower racks halfway through baking. Cool on cookie sheets on wire rack 1 minute. With wide metal spatula, transfer to wire racks to cool completely.

5 Repeat with remaining dough.

EACH COOKIE: ABOUT 30 CALORIES | 0G PROTEIN | 4G CARBOHYDRATE | 2G TOTAL FAT (1G SATURATED) | 0G FIBER | 5MG CHOLESTEROL | 21MG SODIUM

CHECKERBOARD COOKIES

Chocolate and vanilla make up the tasty checkerboard design of these refrigerator squares. The secret is to glue the dough pieces together with milk before chilling them. For additional tips, see Forming & Slicing Checkerboard Dough, opposite.

ACTIVE TIME: 40 MINUTES PLUS CHILLING · **BAKE TIME:** 10 MINUTES PER BATCH
MAKES: 48 COOKIES

2 CUPS ALL-PURPOSE FLOUR	1 LARGE EGG
1 TEASPOON BAKING POWDER	1 TEASPOON VANILLA EXTRACT
¼ TEASPOON SALT	1 SQUARE (1 OUNCE) SEMISWEET CHOCOLATE
½ CUP (1 STICK) PLUS 1 TABLESPOON BUTTER OR MARGARINE, SOFTENED	3 TABLESPOONS UNSWEETENED COCOA
1 CUP SUGAR	MILK FOR ASSEMBLING COOKIES

1 In medium bowl, combine flour, baking powder, and salt. In medium bowl, with mixer at medium speed, beat ½ cup butter and sugar until creamy. Reduce speed to low and beat in egg and vanilla until blended. Beat in flour mixture until combined, scraping bowl occasionally with rubber spatula. Remove half of dough; set aside.

2 In 1-quart saucepan, melt chocolate and remaining 1 tablespoon butter over very low heat. Stir in cocoa until combined. Add chocolate mixture to dough in bowl, stirring until blended.

3 Separately shape chocolate and vanilla doughs into 12" by 2" by 1" blocks. Slice each block lengthwise into two 12" by 1" by 1" strips. Brush one side of 1 chocolate strip with milk; place brushed side next to 1 vanilla strip. Repeat with remaining 2 strips. Brush top of one vanilla/chocolate rectangle with milk. Place second vanilla/chocolate rectangle on top, reversing colors so end forms checkerboard. Wrap block in waxed paper, using paper to square edges. Refrigerate 4 hours or overnight. (If using margarine, freeze overnight.)

4. Preheat oven to 375°F. Grease two large cookie sheets. Cut dough into ¼-inch-thick slices. Place slices, ½-inch apart, on prepared cookie sheets. Bake until golden, 10 to 12 minutes, rotating cookie sheets between upper and lower racks halfway through baking. Cool on cookie sheets on wire racks 5 minutes. With wide metal spatula, transfer to wire racks to cool completely.

EACH COOKIE: ABOUT 60 CALORIES | 1G PROTEIN | 9G CARBOHYDRATE | 2G TOTAL FAT (1G SATURATED) | 0G FIBER | 10MG CHOLESTEROL | 45MG SODIUM

FORMING & SLICING CHECKERBOARD DOUGH

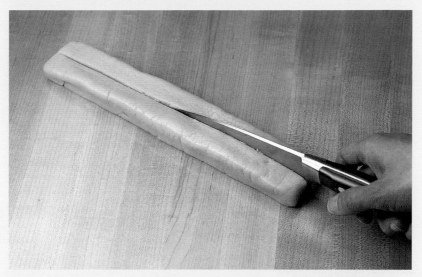

Step 1: Cut each 12 by 2 by 1 block of dough in half lengthwise to make two strips.

Step 2: After dough has been assembled and chilled, slice it into ¼-inch-thick checkerboard cookies.

SPUMONI ICEBOX COOKIES

Contrary to what their name implies, spumoni cookies are not made with ice cream; they only look as if they were. With the help of some red and green paste food coloring, they resemble the popular Italian frozen dessert.

ACTIVE TIME: 55 MINUTES PLUS CHILLING AND COOLING · **BAKE TIME:** 10 MINUTES PER BATCH

MAKES: 90 COOKIES

2¾ CUPS ALL-PURPOSE FLOUR

½ TEASPOON BAKING SODA

⅛ TEASPOON SALT

1 CUP BUTTER OR MARGARINE (2 STICKS), SOFTENED

1 CUP SUGAR

1 LARGE EGG

1 TEASPOON ALMOND EXTRACT

⅓ CUP SHELLED PISTACHIOS (ABOUT ¾ CUP PISTACHIOS IN SHELL), FINELY CHOPPED

GREEN PASTE FOOD COLORING

⅓ CUP RED CANDIED CHERRIES, FINELY CHOPPED

RED PASTE FOOD COLORING

1 Line 9" by 5" metal loaf pan with plastic wrap, letting wrap extend over rim on all sides. On waxed paper, combine flour, baking soda, and salt.

2 In large bowl, with mixer at medium speed, beat butter and sugar 4 minutes or until light and fluffy, occasionally scraping bowl with rubber spatula. Add egg and almond extract and beat until well blended. Reduce speed to low; beat in flour mixture just until blended, occasionally scraping bowl.

3 Transfer 1 rounded cup plain dough to medium bowl; with spoon, stir in pistachios and enough green food coloring to tint dough bright green. In another bowl, place 1 rounded cup plain dough; stir in cherries and enough red food coloring to tint dough bright red.

4 Evenly pat pistachio dough into bottom of prepared pan; freeze 10 minutes. Pat plain dough on top of pistachio layer; freeze 10 minutes. Pat cherry dough on top. Cover pan with plastic wrap and refrigerate 4 hours or overnight, until dough is firm enough to slice.

5 Preheat oven to 350°F. Remove dough from pan; discard plastic wrap. With serrated knife, cut dough crosswise into ¼-inch-thick slices. Cut each slice crosswise into 3 cookies. Place cookies, 2 inches apart, on ungreased large cookie sheet.

6 Bake cookies until firm and golden brown at edges, 10 to 12 minutes. Cool cookies on cookie sheet on wire rack 2 minutes. With wide spatula, carefully transfer cookies to rack to cool completely. Repeat with remaining dough.

EACH COOKIE: ABOUT 45 CALORIES | 1G PROTEIN | 6G CARBOHYDRATE | 3G TOTAL FAT (1G SATURATED) | 0G FIBER | 8MG CHOLESTEROL | 35MG SODIUM

CHOCOLATE ICEBOX COOKIES

You can serve these versatile cookies plain, decorate them with frosting, or make a cookie sandwich filled with jam or melted white chocolate. Crushed, they make a great crust for chocolate cream pie.

ACTIVE TIME: 25 MINUTES PLUS CHILLING · **BAKE TIME:** 10 MINUTES PER BATCH
MAKES: 96 COOKIES

1⅔ CUPS ALL-PURPOSE FLOUR	½ CUP PACKED LIGHT BROWN SUGAR
½ CUP UNSWEETENED COCOA	½ CUP GRANULATED SUGAR
1 TEASPOON BAKING POWDER	2 SQUARES (2 OUNCES) SEMISWEET CHOCOLATE, MELTED AND COOLED
½ TEASPOON BAKING SODA	
¼ TEASPOON SALT	1 TEASPOON VANILLA EXTRACT
¾ CUP BUTTER OR MARGARINE (1½ STICKS), SOFTENED	1 LARGE EGG

1 In medium bowl, stir together flour, cocoa, baking powder, baking soda, and salt.

2 In large bowl, with mixer at medium speed, beat butter and brown and granulated sugars until light and fluffy. Beat in chocolate and vanilla until well combined. Beat in egg. Reduce speed to low and beat in flour mixture until well combined.

3 Divide dough in half. On separate sheets of waxed paper, shape each half into 12" by 1½" log. Wrap each log in the waxed paper (see photo, page 117) and slide onto small cookie sheet for easier handling. Refrigerate dough until firm enough to slice, at least 2 hours or overnight. (If using margarine, freeze overnight.)

4 Preheat oven to 350°F. Cut 1 log crosswise into scant ¼-inch-thick slices; keep remaining log refrigerated. Place slices, 1 inch apart, on two ungreased large cookie sheets. Bake until firm, 10 to 11 minutes, rotating sheets between upper and lower oven racks halfway through baking. Cool on cookie sheets on wire racks 1 minute. With wide metal spatula, transfer to wire racks to cool completely.

5 Repeat with remaining dough.

EACH COOKIE: ABOUT 45 CALORIES | 0G PROTEIN | 5G CARBOHYDRATE | 3G TOTAL FAT (1G SATURATED) | 0G FIBER | 6MG CHOLESTEROL | 31MG SODIUM

OATMEAL ICEBOX COOKIES

The perfect after-school treat, these crisp oatmeal slices can be decorated with raisin, currant, or chocolate chip happy faces before baking. With a roll or two of these in the freezer, you can slice off and bake just what you need, whenever you want.

ACTIVE TIME: 35 MINUTES PLUS CHILLING · **BAKE TIME:** 14 MINUTES PER BATCH
MAKES: 60 COOKIES

1½ CUPS ALL-PURPOSE FLOUR	¾ CUP GRANULATED SUGAR
1 TEASPOON BAKING POWDER	2 LARGE EGGS
½ TEASPOON BAKING SODA	2 TEASPOONS VANILLA EXTRACT
¼ TEASPOON SALT	3 CUPS OLD-FASHIONED OATS, UNCOOKED
1 CUP BUTTER OR MARGARINE (2 STICKS), SOFTENED	1 CUP PECANS (4 OUNCES)
1 CUP PACKED DARK BROWN SUGAR	1 CUP RAISINS

1 On sheet of waxed paper, stir together flour, baking powder, baking soda, and salt until blended.

2 In large bowl, with mixer at medium speed, beat butter and brown and granulated sugars until creamy. Beat in eggs, one at a time, until blended. Beat in vanilla. Reduce speed to low and beat in flour mixture until combined. With wooden spoon, stir in oats, pecans, and raisins.

3 Divide dough in half. On separate sheets of waxed paper, shape each half into 12-inch-long log. Wrap each log in the waxed paper (see photo, page 117) and refrigerate 4 hours or overnight, until firm.

4 Preheat oven to 350°F. With serrated knife, using sawing motion, cut each log crosswise into ⅜-inch-thick slices. Place slices, 2 inches apart, on two ungreased large cookie sheets. Bake 14 minutes, rotating sheets between upper and lower racks halfway through baking, until golden brown. Cool on cookie sheets on wire racks 2 minutes. With wide metal spatula, transfer to wire racks to cool completely.

5 Repeat with remaining cookie dough.

EACH COOKIE: ABOUT 100 CALORIES | 1G PROTEIN | 13G CARBOHYDRATE | 5G TOTAL FAT (2G SATURATED) | 0.5G FIBER | 15MG CHOLESTEROL | 65MG SODIUM

ALMOND ICEBOX COOKIES

With this nut-flavored dough in the freezer, you are never more than fifteen minutes away from fresh homemade cookies.

ACTIVE TIME: 25 MINUTES PLUS CHILLING · **BAKE TIME:** 15 MINUTES PER BATCH
MAKES: 32 COOKIES

1⅓ CUPS ALL-PURPOSE FLOUR	2 LARGE EGGS
2 TEASPOONS BAKING POWDER	½ TEASPOON VANILLA EXTRACT
¼ TEASPOON SALT	¼ TEASPOON ALMOND EXTRACT
½ CUP BUTTER OR MARGARINE (1 STICK), SOFTENED	1 TABLESPOON WATER
¾ CUP SUGAR	32 WHOLE BLANCHED ALMONDS

1 In small bowl, stir together flour, baking powder, and salt. In large bowl, with mixer at medium speed, beat butter and sugar until creamy. Beat in 1 egg and vanilla and almond extracts until blended. Reduce speed to low and beat in flour mixture just until combined, scraping bowl with rubber spatula.

2 On sheet of waxed paper, shape dough into 8" by 1½" log. Wrap in waxed paper (see photo, page 117) and refrigerate until firm enough to slice, 2 hours. (If using margarine, freeze overnight.)

3 Preheat oven to 350°F. Cut log crosswise into ¼-inch-thick slices. Place slices, 1 inch apart, on ungreased large cookie sheet. Whisk together remaining egg and water. Brush cookies with egg glaze. Lightly press 1 almond into the center of each cookie. Bake until lightly browned, 15 minutes. With wide metal spatula, transfer to wire racks to cool completely.

4 Repeat with remaining dough and almonds.

EACH COOKIE: ABOUT 80 CALORIES | 1G PROTEIN | 10G CARBOHYDRATE | 4G TOTAL FAT (2G SATURATED) | 0.5G FIBER | 22MG CHOLESTEROL | 85MG SODIUM

LIME ICEBOX COOKIES

The refreshing flavor of lime creates a delicate cookie. Shaping the dough into rectangles before chilling makes it easier to slice the cookies because the dough rests flat on the cutting board and doesn't lose its shape from the pressure of the knife.

ACTIVE TIME: 30 MINUTES PLUS CHILLING · **BAKE TIME:** 12 MINUTES PER BATCH
MAKES: 48 COOKIES

3   LIMES
½   CUP BUTTER OR MARGARINE
    (1 STICK), SOFTENED
¾   CUP GRANULATED SUGAR

1   LARGE EGG
1¾ CUPS ALL-PURPOSE FLOUR
½   CUP CONFECTIONERS' SUGAR

1   From limes, grate 1 teaspoon peel and squeeze 3 tablespoons juice. In medium bowl, with mixer at medium speed, beat butter and granulated sugar until creamy. Reduce speed to low; beat in egg and lime peel and juice until blended. Beat in flour until combined.

2   Divide dough in half. On separate sheets of waxed paper, shape each half into 6" by 2½" by 1½" brick. Wrap each brick in waxed paper and freeze 3 hours or up to 1 month.

3   Preheat oven to 350°F. Slice 1 brick crosswise into ¼-inch-thick slices. Place slices, 1 inch apart, on ungreased large cookie sheet. Bake until edges are golden brown, 12 to 15 minutes. With wide metal spatula, transfer to wire racks. Sift confectioners' sugar over hot cookies.

4   Repeat with remaining dough and confectioners' sugar.

EACH COOKIE: ABOUT 50 CALORIES | 1G PROTEIN | 8G CARBOHYDRATE | 2G TOTAL FAT
(1G SATURATED) | 0G FIBER | 10MG CHOLESTEROL | 20MG SODIUM

FORTUNE COOKIES

With our homemade fortune cookies, you can have fun personalizing the fortunes for special occasions. The secret to shaping the cookies is to bake only two at a time and to fold them quickly while still hot.

ACTIVE TIME: 45 MINUTES · **BAKE TIME:** 4 MINUTES PER BATCH
MAKES: 14 COOKIES

2   TABLESPOONS BUTTER (DO NOT USE MARGARINE)

¼   CUP CONFECTIONERS' SUGAR

1   LARGE EGG WHITE

1   TEASPOON VANILLA EXTRACT

PINCH SALT

¼   CUP ALL-PURPOSE FLOUR

14 STRIPS PAPER (3" BY ½" EACH) WITH FORTUNES

1 Preheat oven to 375°F. Grease two small cookie sheets.

2 In 1-quart saucepan, heat butter over low heat until melted. Remove saucepan from heat. With wire whisk, beat in confectioners' sugar, egg white, vanilla, and salt until blended. Beat in flour until batter is smooth.

3 Drop 1 heaping teaspoon batter onto cookie sheet. Repeat with another teaspoon batter, at least 4 inches away from first. With small metal spatula or back of spoon, spread batter evenly to form two 3-inch rounds.

4 Bake until cookies are lightly golden, about 4 minutes. Loosen both cookies with metal spatula. Working with 1 cookie at a time, place a fortune across center of hot cookie. Fold hot cookie in half, forming a semicircle, and press edges together. Quickly fold semicircle over edge of small bowl to create fortune-cookie shape. (See Shaping Fortune Cookies, opposite.) Repeat with remaining cookie. Let shaped cookies cool completely on wire rack.

5 Repeat with remaining batter and strips of fortune paper to make 14 cookies in all, cooling cookie sheets between batches and regreasing sheets as necessary.

EACH COOKIE: ABOUT 35 CALORIES | 1G PROTEIN | 4G CARBOHYDRATE | 2G TOTAL FAT (1G SATURATED) | 0G FIBER | 4MG CHOLESTEROL | 30MG SODIUM

SHAPING FORTUNE COOKIES

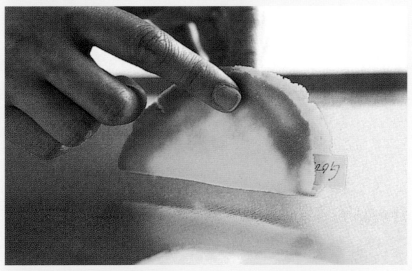

Step 1: After placing a fortune across center of hot cookie, fold cookie in half and press edges together.

Step 2: Immediately fold semicircle over edge of a small bowl to shape.

TULIPES

Place a scoop of ice cream, fresh fruit, or both in these versatile free-form tart shells, and you'll have a memorable dessert. They can be made up to a week ahead.

ACTIVE TIME: 30 MINUTES PLUS COOLING · **BAKE TIME:** 5 MINUTES PER BATCH
MAKES: 12 TULIPES

3	LARGE EGG WHITES	½	TEASPOON VANILLA EXTRACT
¾	CUP CONFECTIONERS' SUGAR	¼	TEASPOON SALT
½	CUP ALL-PURPOSE FLOUR	1	QUART ICE CREAM OR SORBET
6	TABLESPOONS BUTTER, MELTED (DO NOT USE MARGARINE)		

1 Preheat oven to 350°F. Grease large cookie sheet.

2 In large bowl, with wire whisk, beat egg whites, sugar, and flour until blended and smooth. Beat in melted butter, vanilla, and salt.

3 Drop 1 heaping tablespoon batter on prepared cookie sheet. With small metal spatula or back of spoon, spread in circular motion to form 4-inch round. Repeat to make 2 cookies, placing them 4 inches apart. Bake until edges are golden, 5 to 7 minutes.

4 Place two 2-inch-diameter glasses upside down on work surface. With wide metal spatula, quickly lift 1 hot cookie and gently shape over bottom of glass. Shape second cookie. When cookies are cool, transfer to wire rack. If cookies become too firm to shape, return cookie sheet to oven to soften cookies slightly.

5 Repeat Steps 3 and 4 with remaining batter. (Batter will become slightly thicker upon standing.) To serve, place tulipes on dessert plates and fill with a scoop of ice cream.

EACH SERVING WITH ICE CREAM: ABOUT 190 CALORIES | 3G PROTEIN | 22G CARBOHYDRATE | 11G TOTAL FAT (7G SATURATED) | 1G FIBER | 35MG CHOLESTEROL | 155MG SODIUM

HOLIDAY COOKIES

Ever since the seventeenth and eighteenth centuries, when sugar and spices were great luxuries, cookies have been associated with festive occasions. Today, sugar and spices are household staples. Even so, we usually make certain special cookies, many of them beautifully decorated, just once a year, and their aroma is usually the first sign that the holidays are about to begin.

In this chapter, you will find old-world classics, new seasonal ideas from the *Good Housekeeping* kitchens, and personal favorites from our staff and readers. As you select recipes for your holiday baking, we hope some of them will become a part of your family's tradition.

Celebration cookies make welcome gifts, so they often have to travel. You may want to send boxes to friends across the country, pack tins for hostess gifts, or fill a basket for the folks at the office. Here's how to make sure your cookies arrive in perfect condition.

- **When shipping by mail,** choose chewy, soft drop or bar cookies, which travel well. Avoid crisp cookies, which are more likely to break.
- **To wrap,** line a sturdy cardboard box or tin with waxed paper or bubble wrap. Wrap the cookies individually or in pairs, back to back, with plastic wrap.
- **Cushion each layer with crumpled waxed paper,** filling any empty spaces with crumpled paper or bubble wrap, and be sure to mark the wrapped package FRAGILE.
- **When packing cookie assortments for local delivery,** pack them as close to the delivery date as possible to reduce the amount of flavor exchange among the cookies.
- **Pack soft cookies and crisp cookies in separate packages** so that each will retain its ideal texture.

Christmas Fruitcake Drops (page 151)

GINGERBREAD CUTOUTS

Our whimsical ginger people are in good taste any time of the year. At Christmas this spicy dough is perfect for cutting into seasonal shapes or for constructing your own gingerbread house.

ACTIVE TIME: 45 MINUTES PLUS COOLING AND DECORATING
BAKE TIME: 12 MINUTES PER BATCH
MAKES: 36 (3- TO 4-INCH) COOKIES

½ CUP SUGAR

½ CUP LIGHT (MILD) MOLASSES

1½ TEASPOONS GROUND GINGER

1 TEASPOON GROUND ALLSPICE

1 TEASPOON GROUND CINNAMON

1 TEASPOON GROUND CLOVES

2 TEASPOONS BAKING SODA

½ CUP BUTTER OR MARGARINE (1 STICK), CUT INTO PIECES

1 LARGE EGG, BEATEN

3½ CUPS ALL-PURPOSE FLOUR

ORNAMENTAL FROSTING (SEE PAGE 15)

1 In 3-quart saucepan, combine sugar, molasses, ginger, allspice, cinnamon, and cloves over medium heat, stirring occasionally with wooden spoon. When mixture boils, remove pan from heat; stir in baking soda (take care—mixture will foam up in pan). Stir in butter until melted. Stir in egg. Add flour and stir until dough forms.

2 On floured surface, knead dough until combined. Divide dough in half; wrap 1 piece in waxed paper and refrigerate while working with remaining half.

3 Preheat oven to 325°F. On lightly floured surface, with floured rolling pin, roll 1 piece of dough a scant ¼ inch thick. With floured 3- to 4-inch assorted cookie cutters, cut dough into as many cookies as possible; reserve trimmings. Place cookies, 1 inch apart, on ungreased large cookie sheet.

4 Bake until edges begin to brown, 12 minutes. With wide metal spatula, transfer cookies to wire racks to cool. Repeat with remaining dough and trimmings.

5 When cookies are cool, prepare Ornamental Frosting. Use frosting to decorate cookies; let dry completely, about 1 hour.

EACH COOKIE WITHOUT FROSTING: ABOUT 95 CALORIES | 2G PROTEIN | 16G CARBOHYDRATE | 3G TOTAL FAT (2G SATURATED) | 0.5G FIBER | 13MG CHOLESTEROL | 100MG SODIUM

HOLIDAY SUGAR COOKIES

At *Good Housekeeping* we like to use this easy-to-handle dough for any holiday cut-out cookies. It makes a perfect framework for the Holiday Stained-Glass Cookies (see page 140).

ACTIVE TIME: 30 MINUTES PLUS CHILLING · **BAKE TIME:** 10 MINUTES PER BATCH
MAKES: 42 (3-INCH) COOKIES

2¼ CUPS ALL-PURPOSE FLOUR

1½ TEASPOONS BAKING POWDER

¼ TEASPOON SALT

¾ CUP BUTTER OR MARGARINE
(1½ STICKS), SOFTENED

1 CUP SUGAR

1 LARGE EGG

1 TABLESPOON MILK

2 TEASPOONS FRESHLY GRATED LEMON
PEEL OR VANILLA EXTRACT

1 In medium bowl, combine flour, baking powder, and salt. In large bowl, with mixer at medium speed, beat butter and ¾ cup sugar until light and fluffy. Beat in egg, milk, and lemon peel until well combined. Reduce speed to low; beat in flour mixture just until blended. Shape dough into 2 balls; flatten each into disk. Wrap each disk in plastic and refrigerate at least 2 hours or up to overnight.

2 Preheat oven to 350°F. Grease and flour two large cookie sheets. On lightly floured surface, with floured rolling pin, roll 1 disk of dough ⅛ inch thick; keep remaining dough refrigerated. With floured 3-inch assorted cookie cutters, cut dough into as many cookies as possible; reserve trimmings for rerolling. Place cookies, 1 inch apart, on two prepared cookie sheets. If desired, with drinking straw or skewer, make ¼-inch hole in top of each cookie for hanging. Sprinkle some of remaining ¼ cup sugar over cookies.

3 Bake until cookies are golden, about 10 minutes, rotating cookie sheets between upper and lower oven racks halfway through baking. With wide metal spatula, transfer cookies to wire racks to cool completely.

4 Repeat with remaining dough and trimmings.

EACH COOKIE: ABOUT 75 CALORIES | 1G PROTEIN | 10G CARBOHYDRATE | 4G TOTAL FAT
(2G SATURATED) | 0G FIBER | 14MG CHOLESTEROL | 66MG SODIUM

HOLIDAY STAINED-GLASS COOKIES

The crushed hard candy melts in the oven to give these beautiful cookies the look of stained glass. They're pretty enough to hang on your tree.

ACTIVE TIME: 1 HOUR 20 MINUTES · **BAKE TIME:** 10 MINUTES PER BATCH
MAKES: 60 COOKIES

HOLIDAY SUGAR COOKIE DOUGH
(SEE PAGE 139)

1 PACKAGE (10 TO 12 OUNCES) HARD CANDY, SUCH AS SOUR BALLS, IN ASSORTED COLORS (SEE TIP)

1 Prepare Holiday Sugar Cookies dough through Step 1.

2 While dough is chilling, group candies by color and place in separate heavy-duty zip-tight plastic bags. Place 1 bag on towel-covered work surface. With meat mallet or rolling pin, lightly crush candy into small pieces, being careful not to crush until fine and powdery. Repeat with remaining candy.

3 Preheat oven to 350°F. Roll and cut dough as in Step 2 of Holiday Sugar Cookies, but place cut-out cookies on large foil-lined cookie sheet.

4 With mini cookie cutters, canapé cutters, or knife, cut one or more small shapes from each large cookie; remove small cut-out pieces and reserve for rerolling. Place some crushed candy in cutouts of each cookie. With drinking straw, make hole in top of each cookie for hanging. Bake until lightly browned, 10 to 12 minutes. Cool cookies completely on cookie sheet on wire rack.

5 Repeat with remaining dough and trimmings.

6 For wreath, tree, or window decorations, tie ribbons or nylon fishing line through hole in each cookie to make loop for hanging.

TIP Do not use red-and-white-swirled peppermint candies—they won't melt in the oven.

EACH COOKIE: ABOUT 90 CALORIES | 1G PROTEIN | 14G CARBOHYDRATE | 4G TOTAL FAT (1G SATURATED) | 0G FIBER | 7MG CHOLESTEROL | 40MG SODIUM

COCONUT MACAROONS

A traditional Passover sweet, these flourless cookies are delicious any time of the year (and a welcome treat to people who are allergic to wheat or gluten).

ACTIVE TIME: 10 MINUTES · **BAKE TIME:** 25 MINUTES
MAKES: 42 COOKIES

3	CUPS FLAKED SWEETENED COCONUT	¼	TEASPOON SALT
¾	CUP SUGAR	1	TEASPOON VANILLA EXTRACT
4	LARGE EGG WHITES	⅛	TEASPOON ALMOND EXTRACT

1 Preheat oven to 325°F. Line two cookie sheets with cooking parchment or foil.

2 In large bowl, stir coconut, sugar, egg whites, salt, and vanilla and almond extracts until well combined.

3 Drop batter by rounded teaspoons, 1 inch apart, on two prepared cookie sheets. Bake until set and lightly golden, about 25 minutes, rotating cookie sheets between upper and lower oven racks halfway through baking. Cool 1 minute on cookie sheets. With wide metal spatula, transfer cookies to wire racks to cool completely.

EACH COOKIE: ABOUT 40 CALORIES | 1G PROTEIN | 6G CARBOHYDRATE | 2G TOTAL FAT (2G SATURATED) | 0.5G FIBER | 0MG CHOLESTEROL | 32MG SODIUM

CHOCOLATE COCONUT MACAROONS

Prepare as directed, stirring **2 tablespoons unsweetened cocoa** and **1 square (1 ounce) semisweet chocolate,** grated, into coconut mixture in Step 2.

PEPPERMINT MERINGUES

Be sure to check your oven temperature before baking these delicately striped meringues. It is essential to bake them slowly so that they become crisp inside without browning on the outside.

ACTIVE TIME: 15 MINUTES PLUS DRYING · **BAKE TIME:** 2 HOURS
MAKES: 54 MERINGUES

---

4   LARGE EGG WHITES

¼   TEASPOON CREAM OF TARTAR

1   CUP CONFECTIONERS' SUGAR

¼   TEASPOON IMITATION PEPPERMINT EXTRACT (SEE TIP)

RED AND GREEN FOOD COLORING

1   Preheat oven to 225°F. Line two large cookie sheets with foil.

2   In large bowl, with mixer at high speed, beat egg whites and cream of tartar until soft peaks form when beaters are lifted. Gradually sprinkle in sugar, beating until whites stand in stiff, glossy peaks. Beat in peppermint extract.

3   Transfer half of meringue mixture to another bowl. Add enough red food coloring to meringue in one bowl to tint it pale red. Add enough green food coloring to remaining meringue to tint it pale green.

4   Spoon red meringue into large zip-tight plastic bag; cut ¼-inch opening at corner. Repeat with green meringue in separate bag. Fit large decorating bag (we used a 14-inch bag) with basket-weave or large round tip (½-inch- or ¼-inch-diameter opening). Place decorating bag in 2-cup glass measuring cup and fold top third of bag out over top of cup to hold bag wide open. Simultaneously squeeze meringues from both zip-tight bags into decorating bag, filling it no more than two-thirds full with half-red and half-green mixtures.

5   Pipe bicolored meringue onto prepared cookie sheets, leaving 1 inch between each meringue. If using basket-weave tip, pipe 3- to 4-inch-long pleated ribbons; if using round tip, pipe 2-inch rounds. Bake 2 hours. Turn oven off. Leave meringues in oven at least 30 minutes or overnight to dry.

6   Let meringues cool completely before removing from foil with wide metal spatula.

TIP   We found that peppermint extract containing real peppermint oil caused the meringue mixture to quickly deflate. We had good results using imitation peppermint extract, though.

EACH COOKIE: ABOUT 10 CALORIES | 0G PROTEIN | 2G CARBOHYDRATE | 0G TOTAL FAT (0G SATURATED) | 0G FIBER | 0MG CHOLESTEROL | 5MG SODIUM

SALLY ANN COOKIES

These wonderful frosted molasses cookies spiked with coffee were available in Midwestern grocery stores in the 1960s. We adapted the recipe to use butter or margarine in place of lard.

ACTIVE TIME: 1 HOUR PLUS FREEZING AND COOLING · **BAKE TIME:** 15 MINUTES PER BATCH
MAKES: 144 COOKIES

---

1 CUP BUTTER OR MARGARINE (2 STICKS), SOFTENED	2 TEASPOONS GROUND GINGER
1½ CUPS SUGAR	½ TEASPOON GROUND NUTMEG
5½ CUPS ALL-PURPOSE FLOUR	½ TEASPOON SALT
1 CUP LIGHT (MILD) MOLASSES	¼ TEASPOON GROUND CLOVES
½ CUP COLD STRONG COFFEE	SALLY ANN FROSTING (OPPOSITE)
2 TEASPOONS BAKING SODA	HOLIDAY DÉCORS (OPTIONAL)

1 In large bowl, with mixer at low speed, beat and sugar until blended. Increase speed to high; beat until creamy. At low speed, beat in flour, molasses, coffee, baking soda, ginger, nutmeg, salt, and cloves until well blended. Cover bowl with plastic wrap and freeze until firm enough to handle, 1 hour.

2 Divide dough into thirds. On lightly floured surface, shape each third into 12-inch-long log. Wrap each log in plastic and freeze until firm enough to slice, at least 4 hours or overnight.

3 Preheat oven to 350°F. Grease large cookie sheet. Cut 1 log crosswise into ¼-inch-thick slices. Place slices, 1½ inches apart, on prepared cookie sheet. Bake until cookies are set and edges are lightly browned, 15 to 20 minutes. Cool on cookie sheet on wire rack 1 minute. With wide metal spatula, transfer cookies to wire rack to cool completely. Repeat with remaining dough.

4 When cookies are cool, prepare Sally Ann Frosting. With small metal spatula or knife, spread frosting on cookies. If you like, sprinkle cookies with décors. Set cookies aside to allow frosting to dry completely, about 1 hour.

SALLY ANN FROSTING

In 2-quart saucepan, stir **1 cup sugar** and **1 envelope unflavored gelatin** until well mixed. Stir in **1 cup cold water**; heat to boiling over high heat. Reduce heat to low; simmer, uncovered, 10 minutes. Into medium bowl, measure **2 cups confectioners' sugar**. With mixer at low speed, gradually add gelatin mixture to confectioners' sugar until blended. Increase speed to high; beat until smooth and fluffy with an easy spreading consistency, about 10 minutes. Beat in **½ teaspoon vanilla extract**. Keep bowl covered with plastic wrap to prevent frosting from drying out

---

EACH COOKIE WITH FROSTING: ABOUT 55 CALORIES | 0G PROTEIN | 10G CARBOHYDRATE | 1G TOTAL FAT (0G SATURATED) | 0G FIBER | 0MG CHOLESTEROL | 40MG SODIUM

FIGGY BARS

If these bars remind you of an English steamed pudding, it's no accident; that's exactly the flavor we had in mind—complete with a hard-sauce glaze. But we've slashed the fat by formulating this recipe specifically for trans fat–free vegetable oil spread.

ACTIVE TIME: 25 MINUTES PLUS COOLING · **BAKE TIME:** 23 MINUTES PER BATCH
MAKES: 96 BARS

FIGGY BARS

10 OUNCES (SCANT 2 CUPS) DRIED BLACK MISSION FIGS, FINELY CHOPPED

1 CUP WATER

2 CUPS QUICK-COOKING OATS, UNCOOKED

1½ CUPS PACKED BROWN SUGAR

⅔ CUP DARK MOLASSES

6 TABLESPOONS TRANS FAT–FREE VEGETABLE-OIL SPREAD (60% TO 70% OIL)

2 LARGE EGGS

1 CUP ALL-PURPOSE FLOUR

1 CUP TOASTED WHEAT GERM

2 TEASPOONS PUMPKIN-PIE SPICE

2 TEASPOONS FRESHLY GRATED ORANGE PEEL

1 TEASPOON SALT

1 TEASPOON BAKING SODA

1 TEASPOON BAKING POWDER

HARD-SAUCE GLAZE

2 CUPS CONFECTIONERS' SUGAR

⅓ CUP BRANDY

2 TABLESPOONS WARM WATER

1 Preheat oven to 350°F. Lightly spray two 13" by 9" baking pans with non-stick cooking spray. Line both pans with foil, extending foil 2 inches over short sides of pans. Spray foil with cooking spray.

2 In 4-quart saucepan, combine figs and water; heat to boiling over high heat. Remove saucepan from heat; stir in oats. Stir sugar, molasses, and vegetable oil spread into fig mixture until blended. Stir in eggs. Add flour, wheat germ, pumpkin-pie spice, orange peel, salt, baking soda, and baking powder and stir until combined. Divide batter equally between prepared pans; spread evenly.

3 Bake until toothpick inserted in center comes out clean, 23 to 26 minutes. Cool in pans on wire racks 10 minutes.

4 Meanwhile, prepare glaze: In small bowl, stir confectioners' sugar, brandy, and water until blended.

5 Remove pastry from pans by lifting edges of foil; transfer with foil to racks. Brush both hot pastries with glaze. Cool completely.

6 When cool, cut each pastry lengthwise into 4 strips, then cut each strip crosswise into 6 triangles. Store in tightly covered container, with waxed paper between layers, at room temperature up to 1 week or in refrigerator up to 1 month.

EACH BAR: ABOUT 60 CALORIES | 1G PROTEIN | 12G CARBOHYDRATE | 1G TOTAL FAT
(0G SATURATED) | 2G FIBER | 4MG CHOLESTEROL | 50MG SODIUM

PENNSYLVANIA-DUTCH BROWNIES

Just a little bit of chocolate makes these spice bars heavenly. Inspired by the Pennsylvania-Dutch region where chocolate reigns supreme, the delicious results will make you wonder why we haven't all been doing this for years.

ACTIVE TIME: 20 MINUTES PLUS COOLING · **BAKE TIME:** 15 MINUTES

MAKES: 30 BROWNIES

---

4 TABLESPOONS BUTTER OR MARGARINE

1 SQUARE (1 OUNCE) UNSWEETENED CHOCOLATE

¼ CUP LIGHT (MILD) MOLASSES

2 LARGE EGGS

1½ CUPS ALL-PURPOSE FLOUR

1 CUP PLUS 2 TEASPOONS SUGAR

1⅛ TEASPOONS GROUND CINNAMON

1 TEASPOON GROUND GINGER

½ TEASPOON GROUND CLOVES

½ TEASPOON BAKING SODA

½ TEASPOON SALT

1 Preheat oven to 375°F. Grease 13" by 9" baking pan.

2 In 4-quart saucepan, melt butter and chocolate over low heat. Remove from heat.

3 With wire whisk or fork, stir in molasses, then eggs. With spoon, stir in flour, 1 cup sugar, 1 teaspoon cinnamon, ginger, cloves, baking soda, and salt just until blended. Spread batter evenly in pan. Bake until toothpick inserted 2 inches from edge comes out clean, 15 to 20 minutes.

4 Meanwhile, in cup, combine remaining 2 teaspoons sugar and remaining ⅛ teaspoon cinnamon; set aside.

5 Remove pan from oven; immediately sprinkle brownies with cinnamon-sugar mixture. Cool brownies in pan on wire rack at least 2 hours.

6 When cool, cut brownies lengthwise into 3 strips, then cut each strip crosswise into 5 pieces. Cut each piece diagonally in half.

EACH COOKIE: ABOUT 80 CALORIES | 1G PROTEIN | 14G CARBOHYDRATE | 2G TOTAL FAT (1G SATURATED) | 0.5G FIBER | 14MG CHOLESTEROL | 80MG SODIUM

ANGELETTI

Try eating just one of these luscious glazed cookies. They hail from Italy, so consider red, green, and white décors in honor of the country's flag.

ACTIVE TIME: 40 MINUTES PLUS COOLING · **BAKE TIME:** 7 MINUTES PER BATCH
MAKES: 60 COOKIES

½ CUP BUTTER OR MARGARINE (1 STICK), MELTED

¾ CUP GRANULATED SUGAR

¼ CUP WHOLE MILK

1½ TEASPOONS VANILLA EXTRACT

3 LARGE EGGS

3 CUPS ALL-PURPOSE FLOUR

1 TABLESPOON BAKING POWDER

¼ TEASPOON SALT

2 CUPS CONFECTIONERS' SUGAR

3½ TABLESPOONS WATER

½ CUP MULTICOLOR CANDY DÉCORS

1 Preheat oven to 375°F. Grease large cookie sheet.

2 In large bowl, whisk butter, granulated sugar, milk, vanilla, and eggs until blended. In medium bowl, mix flour, baking powder, and salt. Stir flour mixture into egg mixture until evenly blended. Cover dough with plastic wrap or waxed paper; let stand 5 minutes.

3 With floured hands, shape dough by level tablespoons into 1-inch balls. Place balls, 2 inches apart, on prepared cookie sheet. Bake until puffed and light brown on bottoms, 7 to 8 minutes. With wide metal spatula, transfer cookies to wire rack to cool. Repeat with remaining dough.

4 When cookies are cool, in small bowl, whisk confectioners' sugar and water until blended. Dip top of each cookie into glaze. Place cookies on wire rack set over waxed paper to catch any drips. Immediately sprinkle cookies with décors. Allow glaze to set, about 20 minutes.

EACH COOKIE: ABOUT 75 CALORIES | 1G PROTEIN | 13G CARBOHYDRATE | 2G TOTAL FAT (1G SATURATED) | 0G FIBER | 15MG CHOLESTEROL | 55MG SODIUM

MOSTACCIOLI

The origin of these classic Italian cookies can be traced back to the ancient Romans, who made small cakes known as *"mustacae."*

ACTIVE TIME: 45 MINUTES PLUS COOLING · **BAKE TIME:** 7 MINUTES PER BATCH
MAKES: 60 COOKIES

2   CUPS ALL-PURPOSE FLOUR

½   CUP PLUS 3 TABLESPOONS UNSWEETENED COCOA, PLUS MORE FOR ROLLING

1½ TEASPOONS BAKING POWDER

1   TEASPOON GROUND CINNAMON

¼   TEASPOON GROUND CLOVES

¼   TEASPOON SALT

¾   CUP GRANULATED SUGAR

½   CUP BUTTER OR MARGARINE (1 STICK), SOFTENED

1   LARGE EGG

½   CUP MILK

¼   CUP BOILING WATER

1¼ CUPS CONFECTIONERS' SUGAR

WHITE CANDY DÉCORS FOR GARNISH

1 Preheat oven to 400°F. In medium bowl, combine flour, ½ cup cocoa, baking powder, cinnamon, cloves, and salt. In large bowl, with mixer at low speed, beat granulated sugar and butter until blended, occasionally scraping bowl with rubber spatula. Increase speed to high; beat until light and creamy. At low speed, beat in egg. Alternately beat in flour mixture and milk, beginning and ending with flour mixture, just until combined, occasionally scraping bowl.

2 With cocoa-dusted hands, shape dough by level tablespoons into 1-inch balls. Place balls, 2 inches apart, on ungreased large cookie sheet. Bake until puffed, 7 to 9 minutes (they will look dry and slightly cracked). With wide metal spatula, transfer cookies to wire rack to cool completely. Repeat with remaining dough.

3 When cookies are cool, in small bowl, with wire whisk or fork, gradually mix boiling water into remaining 3 tablespoons cocoa until smooth. Gradually stir in confectioners' sugar and blend well. Dip top of each cookie into glaze. Place cookies on wire rack set over waxed paper to catch any drips. Immediately sprinkle cookies with décors. Allow glaze to set, about 20 minutes.

EACH COOKIE: ABOUT 55 CALORIES | 1G PROTEIN | 9G CARBOHYDRATE | 2G TOTAL FAT (1G SATURATED) | 0.5G FIBER | 8MG CHOLESTEROL | 40MG SODIUM

CHRISTMAS FRUITCAKE DROPS

An irresistible combination of coconut, chocolate, prunes, and cherries. For photo, see page 136.

ACTIVE TIME: 30 MINUTES PLUS COOLING · **BAKE TIME:** 10 MINUTES PER BATCH

MAKES: 36 COOKIES

1¾ CUPS ALL-PURPOSE FLOUR

½ TEASPOON BAKING SODA

¼ TEASPOON SALT

1 CUP PACKED LIGHT BROWN SUGAR

6 TABLESPOONS BUTTER OR MARGARINE, SOFTENED

2 TABLESPOONS VEGETABLE SHORTENING

1 LARGE EGG

1 CUP PITTED PRUNES, COARSELY CHOPPED

1 CUP GOLDEN RAISINS

½ CUP RED CANDIED CHERRIES, COARSELY CHOPPED

½ CUP FLAKED SWEETENED COCONUT

3 SQUARES OR 1 BAR (3 OUNCES) WHITE CHOCOLATE, CHOPPED

1 Preheat oven to 375°F. Grease large cookie sheet. In large bowl, combine flour, baking soda, and salt.

2 In another large bowl, with mixer at low speed, beat brown sugar, butter, and shortening until blended, occasionally scraping bowl with rubber spatula. Increase speed to high; beat until creamy, about 2 minutes. At low speed, beat in egg until blended. Add flour mixture, prunes, raisins, cherries, and coconut, and beat just until blended.

3 Drop dough by rounded tablespoons, about 2 inches apart, on prepared cookie sheet. Bake until edges are golden, 10 to 12 minutes (cookies will be soft). With wide metal spatula, transfer cookies to wire rack to cool. Repeat with remaining dough.

4 In heavy small saucepan, melt white chocolate over very low heat, stirring frequently, until smooth. On sheet of waxed paper, arrange cookies in single layer. Using spoon, drizzle white chocolate over cookies. Allow white chocolate to set, refrigerating if necessary.

EACH COOKIE: ABOUT 130 CALORIES | 1G PROTEIN | 22G CARBOHYDRATE | 4G TOTAL FAT (2G SATURATED) | 1G FIBER | 6MG CHOLESTEROL | 70MG SODIUM

SPRITZ COOKIES

Making these buttery molded favorites is easy with one of the new cookie presses. You will find cookie patterns for every holiday, and this dough will work for all of them!

ACTIVE TIME: 15 MINUTES · **BAKE TIME:** 10 MINUTES PER BATCH
MAKES: 60 COOKIES

1 CUP BUTTER OR MARGARINE (2 STICKS), SOFTENED	⅛ TEASPOON ALMOND EXTRACT
¾ CUP CONFECTIONERS' SUGAR	2 CUPS ALL-PURPOSE FLOUR
1 TEASPOON VANILLA EXTRACT	⅛ TEASPOON SALT

1 Preheat oven to 350°F. In large bowl, with mixer at medium speed, beat butter and confectioners' sugar until light and fluffy. Beat in vanilla and almond extracts. Reduce speed to low; add flour and salt and beat until well combined.

2 Spoon one-third of dough into cookie press fitted with pattern of choice. Press cookies, 1 inch apart, on two ungreased cookie sheets.

3 Bake until edges are golden brown, 10 to 12 minutes, rotating cookie sheets between upper and lower oven racks halfway through baking. With wide metal spatula, transfer cookies to wire racks to cool completely.

4 Repeat with remaining dough.

EACH COOKIE: ABOUT 50 CALORIES | 0G PROTEIN | 5G CARBOHYDRATE | 3G TOTAL FAT (2G SATURATED) | 0G FIBER | 8MG CHOLESTEROL | 36MG SODIUM

CHOCOLATE SPRITZ COOKIES

Prepare as directed but use **1 cup confectioners' sugar**. Add **2 squares (2 ounces) unsweetened chocolate,** chopped, melted, and cooled, after beating butter and sugar.

ALMOND SPRITZ COOKIES

In food processor with knife blade attached, process **¾ cup whole natural almonds,** toasted (see page 75), and **¼ cup confectioners' sugar** until nuts are finely ground. Prepare as directed, using **¼ teaspoon almond extract** and **2¼ cups all-purpose flour**. Add ground almonds. Dough will be quite stiff. Makes about 72 cookies.

GREEK CHRISTMAS COOKIES

These colorful spice cookies are a delightful addition to any celebration.

ACTIVE TIME: 50 MINUTES · **BAKE TIME:** 15 MINUTES PER BATCH
MAKES: 72 COOKIES

1	CUP BUTTER OR MARGARINE (2 STICKS), SOFTENED	½	TEASPOON GROUND CLOVES
2	CUPS CONFECTIONERS' SUGAR	⅛	TEASPOON SALT
2	CUPS ALL-PURPOSE FLOUR	1	LARGE EGG YOLK
1	TEASPOON GROUND CINNAMON	2	CUPS BLANCHED ALMONDS, GROUND
½	TEASPOON GROUND NUTMEG		ABOUT 1 CUP RED CANDIED CHERRIES, EACH CUT IN HALF

1 Preheat oven to 350°F. In large bowl, with mixer at low speed, beat butter and confectioners' sugar until blended. Increase speed to high; beat until light and creamy. At low speed, beat in flour, cinnamon, nutmeg, cloves, salt, and egg yolk. With hands, knead in almonds.

2 Roll dough into 1-inch balls (dough will be crumbly). Place balls, about 2 inches apart, on ungreased large cookie sheet. Gently press a cherry half on top of each ball. Bake until bottoms of cookies are lightly browned, 15 minutes. With wide metal spatula, transfer cookies to wire rack to cool.

3 Repeat with remaining dough and cherries.

EACH COOKIE: ABOUT 75 CALORIES | 1G PROTEIN | 9G CARBOHYDRATE | 4G TOTAL FAT (1G SATURATED) | 0G FIBER | 3MG CHOLESTEROL | 40MG SODIUM

CZECHOSLOVAKIAN COOKIES

Kids will love assembling the strawberry and walnut layers of these traditional Christmas cookies in the baking pan.

ACTIVE TIME: 25 MINUTES · **BAKE TIME:** 45 MINUTES
MAKES: 30 BARS

---

1 CUP BUTTER (2 STICKS), SOFTENED (DO NOT USE MARGARINE)	2 CUPS ALL-PURPOSE FLOUR
1 CUP SUGAR	⅛ TEASPOON SALT
2 LARGE EGG YOLKS	1 CUP WALNUTS (4 OUNCES), CHOPPED
	½ CUP STRAWBERRY PRESERVES

1 Preheat oven to 350°F. Grease 9-inch square baking pan.

2 In large bowl, with mixer at low speed, beat butter and sugar until mixed, occasionally scraping bowl with rubber spatula. Increase speed to high; beat until light and fluffy. Reduce speed to low and beat in egg yolks until well combined, constantly scraping bowl with rubber spatula. Add flour and salt; beat until blended, occasionally scraping bowl. With wooden spoon, stir in chopped walnuts.

3 With lightly floured hands, divide dough in half. Pat 1 piece of dough evenly into bottom of prepared pan. Spread strawberry preserves over dough. With lightly floured hands, pinch off ¾-inch pieces from remaining dough and drop over preserves; do not pat down.

4 Bake until golden, 45 to 50 minutes. Cool completely in pan on wire rack. When cool, cut lengthwise into 3 strips, then cut each strip crosswise into 10 pieces.

EACH COOKIE: ABOUT 130 CALORIES | 2G PROTEIN | 11G CARBOHYDRATE | 9G TOTAL FAT (4G SATURATED) | 0.5G FIBER | 31MG CHOLESTEROL | 70MG SODIUM

Clockwise from top right: Wooden-Spoon Cookies (page 156),
Hazelnut Sandwich Cookies (page 158), Czechoslovakian Cookies

WOODEN-SPOON COOKIES

The handle of a wooden spoon gives these cookies their delightful arch. Be sure to bake only a few at a time so you will be able to roll each cookie around the spoon handle before the cookies cool.

ACTIVE TIME: 25 MINUTES · **BAKE TIME:** 5 MINUTES PER BATCH
MAKES: 36 COOKIES

¾ CUP BLANCHED ALMONDS, GROUND

½ CUP BUTTER OR MARGARINE (1 STICK), SOFTENED

½ CUP SUGAR

1 TABLESPOON ALL-PURPOSE FLOUR

1 TABLESPOON HEAVY OR WHIPPING CREAM

1 Preheat oven to 350°F. Grease and flour two large cookie sheets. In 2-quart saucepan, combine ground almonds, butter, sugar, flour, and cream. Heat over low heat, stirring occasionally, until butter melts. Keep mixture warm over very low heat.

2 Drop batter by rounded teaspoons, about 3 inches apart, on two prepared cookie sheets. (Do not place more than 6 on each cookie sheet because, after baking, cookies must be shaped quickly before hardening.)

3 Bake until edges are lightly browned and centers are just golden, 5 to 7 minutes, rotating sheets between upper and lower oven racks halfway through baking.

4 Cool on cookie sheets until edges are just set, 30 to 60 seconds. With wide metal spatula or long, flexible metal spatula, flip cookies over quickly so lacy texture will be on outside after rolling. Working as swiftly as possible, roll cookies, one at a time, into cylinder around handle of wooden spoon (see photos of technique, page 45); transfer to wire rack. (If cookies become too hard to roll, reheat on cookie sheet in oven 1 minute to soften.) As each cookie is shaped, remove from spoon handle; cool on wire rack.

5 Repeat with remaining batter.

EACH COOKIE: ABOUT 50 CALORIES | 1G PROTEIN | 3G CARBOHYDRATE | 4G TOTAL FAT (1G SATURATED) | 0.5G FIBER | 1MG CHOLESTEROL | 35MG SODIUM

SAND TARTS

Pennsylvania bakers used to compete to see who could make the thinnest, crispest sand tarts.

ACTIVE TIME: 1 HOUR, 30 MINUTES PLUS CHILLING · **BAKE TIME:** 12 MINUTES PER BATCH
MAKES: 72 COOKIES

1	CUP BUTTER (2 STICKS), SOFTENED (DO NOT USE MARGARINE)	
1½	CUPS SUGAR	
2	LARGE EGGS	
1	TEASPOON VANILLA EXTRACT	

3 CUPS ALL-PURPOSE FLOUR
½ TEASPOON BAKING POWDER
½ TEASPOON SALT
ORNAMENTAL FROSTING (OPTIONAL, SEE PAGE 15)

1 In large bowl, with mixer at low speed, beat butter and sugar until blended. Increase speed to high; beat until light and creamy. At low speed, beat in eggs and vanilla until mixed. Beat in flour, baking powder, and salt until well combined, occasionally scraping bowl with rubber spatula. Shape dough into 4 balls; flatten each slightly. Wrap each ball of dough in plastic wrap and freeze until dough is firm enough to roll, at least 1 hour, or refrigerate overnight.

2 Preheat oven to 350°F. On lightly floured surface, with floured rolling pin, roll 1 piece of dough slightly thinner than ¼ inch; keep remaining dough refrigerated. With floured 3- to 4-inch assorted cookie cutters, cut dough into as many cookies as possible; reserve trimmings. Place cookies, about 1 inch apart, on ungreased large cookie sheet.

3 Bake until edges are golden, 12 to 15 minutes. With wide metal spatula, transfer cookies to wire rack to cool. Repeat with remaining dough and trimmings.

4 When cookies are cool, if you like, prepare Ornamental Frosting. Use to decorate cookie as desired, then set cookies aside to allow frosting to dry completely, about 1 hour.

EACH COOKIE WITH FROSTING: ABOUT 60 CALORIES | 1G PROTEIN | 8G CARBOHYDRATE | 3G TOTAL FAT (2G SATURATED) | 0G FIBER | 13MG CHOLESTEROL | 45MG SODIUM

HAZELNUT SANDWICH COOKIES

Be patient: No matter how eager you are to eat them, the baking of these hazelnut meringues can't be hurried.

ACTIVE TIME: 1 HOUR PLUS COOLING · **BAKE TIME:** 25 MINUTES PER BATCH
MAKES: 48 SANDWICH COOKIES

2   CUPS HAZELNUTS (FILBERTS, 10 OUNCES)

¾   CUP SUGAR

5   LARGE EGG WHITES

⅓ CUP ALL-PURPOSE FLOUR

5   TABLESPOONS BUTTER OR MARGARINE, MELTED AND COOLED

6   SQUARES (6 OUNCES) SEMISWEET CHOCOLATE, MELTED AND COOLED

1   Preheat oven to 350°F. Toast and skin hazelnuts (see page 75).

2   Turn oven control to 275°F. Grease two large cookie sheets. In food processor with knife blade attached, process hazelnuts and ¼ cup sugar until nuts are finely ground.

3   In large bowl, with mixer at high speed, beat egg whites until soft peaks form when beaters are lifted. Increase speed to high and sprinkle in remaining ½ cup sugar, 1 tablespoon at a time, beating well after each addition, until sugar has completely dissolved and whites stand in stiff peaks. With rubber spatula, fold in ground hazelnuts, flour, and melted margarine.

4   Drop mixture by rounded teaspoons, about 2 inches apart, onto two prepared cookie sheets. Bake until cookies are firm and edges are golden, 25 minutes, rotating cookie sheets between upper and lower racks halfway through baking time. With wide metal spatula, transfer to wire racks to cool. Repeat with remaining batter.

5   When cookies are cool, with small metal spatula, spread thin layer of melted chocolate onto flat side of half of cookies. Top with remaining cookies, flat side down, to make sandwiches. Spoon remaining chocolate into small zip-tight plastic bag; snip 1 corner of bag to make small hole. Squeeze thin lines of chocolate over cookies. Let stand until set.

EACH SANDWICH COOKIE: ABOUT 75 CALORIES | 1G PROTEIN | 7G CARBOHYDRATE | 5G TOTAL FAT (0G SATURATED) | 1G FIBER | 0MG CHOLESTEROL | 25MG SODIUM

MOLASSES LACE ROLLS

These ladylike cookies add a touch of elegance to any holiday party.

ACTIVE TIME: 30 MINUTES · **BAKE TIME:** 8 MINUTES PER BATCH
MAKES: 42 COOKIES

½ CUP LIGHT (MILD) MOLASSES

½ CUP BUTTER (1 STICK, DO NOT USE MARGARINE)

½ CUP SUGAR

1 CUP ALL-PURPOSE FLOUR

½ TEASPOON BAKING POWDER

¼ TEASPOON BAKING SODA

1 Preheat oven to 350°F. Grease large cookie sheet.

2 In 2-quart saucepan, heat molasses, butter, and sugar to boiling over medium heat, stirring often; boil 1 minute. Remove saucepan from heat; gradually stir in flour, baking powder, and baking soda until combined. Place saucepan in skillet of hot water to keep batter warm.

3 Drop batter by heaping teaspoons, 3 inches apart, onto prepared cookie sheet. (Do not place more than 6 on cookie sheet because, after baking, cookies must be shaped quickly before hardening.) Bake until lacy and lightly browned, 8 minutes.

4 Cool on cookie sheet on wire rack until cookies are set slightly, about 1 minute. With wide metal spatula, quickly loosen and turn cookies over. Working as quickly as possible, roll cookies one at a time around handle of wooden spoon. (If cookies become too hard to roll, reheat on cookie sheet in oven 1 minute to soften.) As each cookie is shaped, remove from spoon handle; cool on wire rack.

5 Repeat with remaining batter.

EACH COOKIE: ABOUT 50 CALORIES | 0G PROTEIN | 7G CARBOHYDRATE | 2G TOTAL FAT (1G SATURATED) | 0G FIBER | 6MG CHOLESTEROL | 35MG SODIUM

GRANDMA'S CRESCENTS

This versatile cookie is a Ukranian Christmas treat. It can be filled with any fruit preserves or with almond paste instead of prune butter.

ACTIVE TIME: 1 HOUR 15 MINUTES PLUS CHILLING · **BAKE TIME:** 25 MINUTES PER BATCH
MAKES: 48 COOKIES

---

1 CUP WALNUTS (4 OUNCES), TOASTED (SEE PAGE 75)

½ CUP PLUS 2 TABLESPOONS GRANULATED SUGAR

3¼ CUPS ALL-PURPOSE FLOUR

2½ TEASPOONS BAKING POWDER

½ TEASPOON SALT

1 CUP COLD BUTTER (2 STICKS), CUT INTO PIECES (DO NOT USE MARGARINE)

2 LARGE EGGS

1 TEASPOON ALMOND EXTRACT

⅓ CUP PLUS 2 TABLESPOONS MILK

1 JAR (17 OUNCES) PRUNE BUTTER (LEKVAR; ABOUT 1½ CUPS)

CONFECTIONERS' SUGAR

1 In food processor with knife blade attached, process nuts and ¼ cup granulated sugar until finely ground. Add flour, baking powder, and salt; pulse to blend. Add butter; pulse until coarse crumbs form. Add eggs, almond extract, and ⅓ cup milk and pulse just until dough forms and pulls away from side of bowl. Pat into a ball. Divide into 6 pieces. Wrap each with plastic and refrigerate at least 2 hours or overnight.

2 Preheat oven to 350°F. In medium bowl, mix prune butter and ¼ cup granulated sugar. Grease two large cookie sheets.

3 On floured surface, with floured rolling pin, roll 1 piece dough into 9-inch round; keep remaining dough chilled. Spread round with ¼ cup filling. With sharp knife, cut into 8 wedges. Starting at curved edge, roll each wedge, jelly-roll fashion. Place cookies, pointed end down, 2 inches apart, on prepared sheet. Repeat with 2 more pieces of dough.

4 With pastry brush, brush crescents with milk; sprinkle with granulated sugar. Bake until golden, 25 minutes, rotating cookie sheets between upper and lower racks halfway through. Immediately transfer crescents to wire rack to cool.

6 Repeat with remaining 3 pieces of dough. Sprinkle with confectioners' sugar before serving.

EACH COOKIE: ABOUT 110 CALORIES | 2G PROTEIN | 13G CARBOHYDRATE | 6G TOTAL FAT (3G SATURATED) | 1G FIBER | 19MG CHOLESTEROL | 105MG SODIUM

CREAM CHEESE–WALNUT COOKIES

These rich cookies are made with just six ingredients! You can decorate them with colored sugar or sprinkles.

ACTIVE TIME: 30 MINUTES · **BAKE TIME:** 14 MINUTES PER BATCH

MAKES: 60 COOKIES

½ CUP BUTTER OR MARGARINE (1 STICK), SOFTENED

1 SMALL PACKAGE (3 OUNCES) CREAM CHEESE, SOFTENED

1 CUP SUGAR

1 TEASPOON VANILLA EXTRACT

1 CUP ALL-PURPOSE FLOUR

½ CUP WALNUTS, FINELY CHOPPED

1 Preheat oven to 350°F. In large bowl, with mixer at low speed, beat butter, cream cheese, and sugar until blended. Increase speed to high; beat until creamy, about 2 minutes, scraping bowl with rubber spatula. Beat in vanilla. With wooden spoon, stir in flour and walnuts just until blended.

2 With lightly floured hands, roll dough into 1-inch balls. Place balls, 2 inches apart, on ungreased large cookie sheet. With floured fingertips, flatten balls into 1¼-inch rounds. Bake until golden, 14 to 18 minutes. Let cool on cookie sheet on wire rack 2 minutes. With wide metal spatula, transfer cookies to wire rack to cool completely.

3 Repeat with remaining dough.

EACH COOKIE: ABOUT 45 CALORIES | 1G PROTEIN | 5G CARBOHYDRATE | 3G TOTAL FAT (1G SATURATED) | 0G FIBER | 2MG CHOLESTEROL | 25MG SODIUM

HAMANTASCHEN

In Jewish homes, hamantaschen are served for Purim. These three-cornered pastries can be made with either prune or poppy-seed filling.

ACTIVE TIME: 1 HOUR PLUS CHILLING · **BAKE TIME:** 12 MINUTES PER BATCH
MAKES: 42 COOKIES

2 CUPS ALL-PURPOSE FLOUR	1 LARGE EGG
¾ TEASPOON BAKING POWDER	1 LARGE EGG YOLK
⅛ TEASPOON SALT	1 TEASPOON VANILLA EXTRACT
1 LEMON	1 JAR (17 OUNCES) PRUNE BUTTER (LEKVAR; ABOUT 1½ CUPS)
½ CUP BUTTER OR MARGARINE (1 STICK), SOFTENED	4 TEASPOONS PACKED LIGHT BROWN SUGAR
⅔ CUP GRANULATED SUGAR	

1 In medium bowl, stir together flour, baking powder, and salt. From lemon, grate 1 teaspoon peel and squeeze 1 teaspoon juice.

2 In large bowl, with mixer at medium speed, beat butter until creamy. Beat in granulated sugar until light and fluffy. Beat in egg, egg yolk, vanilla, and ½ teaspoon lemon peel until combined. Reduce speed to low and beat in flour mixture until combined. Divide dough in half. Wrap each half in waxed paper and refrigerate several hours or overnight.

3 Preheat oven to 375°F. Line two large cookie sheets with foil. In small bowl, stir together prune butter, brown sugar, lemon juice, and remaining ½ teaspoon lemon peel.

4 On lightly floured surface, with floured rolling pin, roll 1 piece of dough ⅛ inch thick; keep remaining dough refrigerated. With 2½-inch round biscuit cutter, cut 20 rounds; reserve trimmings.

5 Spoon 1 teaspoon prune mixture into center of each round. To make triangular pocket, lift edge of dough at three points and pinch together, partially covering filling. (See Forming Hamantaschen, opposite.) Place 1 inch apart on prepared cookie sheets.

6 Bake, 1 sheet at a time, 12 minutes, or until pastries are lightly browned. Cool 1 minute on cookie sheet on wire rack. With wide metal spatula, transfer to wire rack to cool completely.

7 Repeat with remaining dough, trimmings, and filling.

EACH COOKIE: ABOUT 95 CALORIES | 1G PROTEIN | 17G CARBOHYDRATE | 2G TOTAL FAT (1G SATURATED) | 0.5G FIBER | 16MG CHOLESTEROL | 45 MG SODIUM

FORMING HAMANTASCHEN

Step 1: To fill the hamantaschen, spoon 1 teaspoon of the prune butter (lekvar) into the center of each dough round.

Step 2: To shape the three-cornered "hats," lift the edge of the dough at three points and pinch together, partially covering the filling.

NUT CRESCENTS

There are many variations of these buttery, ground-nut cookies. Lightly toasting the almonds or hazelnuts intensifies the nutty flavor.

ACTIVE TIME: 45 MINUTES PLUS CHILLING · **BAKE TIME:** 20 MINUTES PER BATCH
MAKES: 72 COOKIES

1 CUP BLANCHED WHOLE ALMONDS OR HAZELNUTS (FILBERTS), LIGHTLY TOASTED (SEE PAGE 75)	2 CUPS ALL-PURPOSE FLOUR
	1 TEASPOON ALMOND EXTRACT
½ CUP GRANULATED SUGAR	½ TEASPOON VANILLA EXTRACT
¼ TEASPOON SALT	¾ CUP CONFECTIONERS' SUGAR
1 CUP BUTTER (2 STICKS), SOFTENED (DO NOT USE MARGARINE)	

1 In food processor with knife blade attached, process nuts, ¼ cup granulated sugar, and salt until nuts are very finely ground.

2 In large bowl, with mixer at low speed, beat butter and remaining ¼ cup granulated sugar until blended, occasionally scraping bowl with rubber spatula. Increase speed to high; beat until light and fluffy, about 3 minutes. Reduce speed to low. Gradually add flour, ground-nut mixture, and almond and vanilla extracts; beat until blended. Divide dough in half. Wrap each piece in plastic and refrigerate until dough is firm enough to handle, about 1 hour, or freeze about 30 minutes.

3 Preheat oven to 325°F. Working with 1 piece of dough at a time, with lightly floured hands, shape rounded teaspoons of dough into 2 by ½" crescents. Place crescents, 1 inch apart, on two ungreased cookie sheets.

4 Bake until edges are lightly browned, about 20 minutes, rotating cookie sheets between upper and lower oven racks halfway through baking. With wide metal spatula, transfer cookies to wire racks set over waxed paper. Immediately dust confectioners' sugar over cookies until well coated; cool completely.

5 Repeat with remaining dough.

EACH COOKIE: ABOUT 60 CALORIES | 1G PROTEIN | 6G CARBOHYDRATE | 4G TOTAL FAT (2G SATURATED) | 0.5G FIBER | 7MG CHOLESTEROL | 34MG SODIUM

PALMIERS

Making these crisp, flaky pastries is a snap with our easy four-ingredient recipe. The dough can be completely shaped ahead and refrigerated for up to one week or frozen for up to three. Then simply slice and bake the palmiers when you need them.

ACTIVE TIME: 35 MINUTES PLUS CHILLING · **BAKE TIME:** 15 MINUTES PER BATCH
MAKES: 112 COOKIES

1½ CUPS COLD BUTTER (3 STICKS), CUT INTO PIECES (DO NOT USE MARGARINE)

3 CUPS ALL-PURPOSE FLOUR

¾ CUP SOUR CREAM

1 CUP SUGAR

1 In large bowl, with pastry blender or two knives used scissor-fashion, cut butter into flour until mixture resembles coarse crumbs. Stir in sour cream. On lightly floured surface, knead dough just until it holds together; flatten into 8 by 6 rectangle. Wrap in plastic wrap and refrigerate overnight.

2 Preheat oven to 400°F. Sprinkle ½ cup sugar evenly over work surface. Cut dough in half. With lightly floured rolling pin, on sugared surface, roll 1 piece of dough into 14-inch square; keep remaining dough refrigerated. Using side of your hand or fingertips, make indentation down along center of dough. Starting from one side, tightly roll dough up to indentation. Roll up other side of dough until it meets first roll, incorporating as much sugar as possible into dough; refrigerate. Repeat with remaining piece of dough and remaining ½ cup sugar.

3 With serrated knife, cut dough scroll crosswise into ¼-inch-thick slices. Return dough to refrigerator for a few minutes if too soft to slice. (See Rolling & Cutting Palmiers, opposite.) Place slices, 2 inches apart, on ungreased cookie sheet. Bake 10 minutes. With wide metal spatula, carefully turn cookies over and bake until sugar has caramelized and cookies are a deep golden color, about 5 minutes longer. Cool 1 minute on cookie sheet; then, with wide metal spatula, transfer cookies to wire racks to cool completely.

4 Repeat slicing, baking, and cooling with remaining dough scroll.

EACH COOKIE: ABOUT 45 CALORIES | 1G PROTEIN | 4G CARBOHYDRATE | 3G TOTAL FAT (2G SATURATED) | 0G FIBER | 7MG CHOLESTEROL | 26MG SODIUM

ROLLING & CUTTING PALMIERS

Step 1: Roll up dough from each side of 14-inch square to meet at a mark in the center. Incorporate as much sugar as possible.

Step 2: Cut shaped dough crosswise into ¼-inch-thick slices with a serrated knife. If the dough seems soft, chill it before cutting.

BROWNED-BUTTER SHORTBREAD

To give the shortbread a rich, nutty flavor, we used an old Scottish baking trick—we lightly browned some of the butter.

ACTIVE TIME: 15 MINUTES PLUS CHILLING · **BAKE TIME:** 40 MINUTES
MAKES: 16 WEDGES

¾ CUP UNSALTED BUTTER (1½ STICKS), SLIGHTLY SOFTENED (DO NOT USE MARGARINE)

½ CUP SUGAR

1¾ CUPS ALL-PURPOSE FLOUR

½ TEASPOON SALT

1 In heavy 2-quart saucepan, melt 6 tablespoons butter over low heat. Cook butter, stirring occasionally, until solids at bottom of pan are a rich brown color and butter has a nutty aroma, 8 to 12 minutes. (Be careful not to overbrown butter; it will become bitter.) Pour browned butter into small bowl; refrigerate until almost firm, about 35 minutes.

2 Preheat oven to 350°F. In large bowl, with mixer at medium speed, beat sugar, cooled browned butter, and remaining 6 tablespoons softened butter until creamy.

3 Mix flour and salt into butter mixture by hand just until crumbs form. (Do not overwork dough; shortbread will turn out tough.) Pat shortbread crumbs onto bottom of ungreased 9-inch round tart pan with removable bottom.

4 Bake shortbread until browned around edge, 40 to 45 minutes. Cool in pan on wire rack 10 minutes.

5 Carefully remove side of pan and transfer shortbread to cutting board. While still warm, cut shortbread into 16 wedges. Cool wedges completely on wire rack.

EACH COOKIE: ABOUT 150 CALORIES | 2G PROTEIN | 17G CARBOHYDRATE | 9G TOTAL FAT (5G SATURATED) | 0.5G FIBER | 23MG CHOLESTEROL | 70MG SODIUM

BROWN SUGAR–PECAN SHORTBREAD

These delicious shortbread wedges make wonderful gifts. They will keep for up to a week in a tightly covered tin at room temperature and up to three months frozen.

ACTIVE TIME: 20 MINUTES · **BAKE TIME:** 23 MINUTES
MAKES: 24 WEDGES

¾ CUP UNSALTED BUTTER
(1½ STICKS), SLIGHTLY SOFTENED
(DO NOT USE MARGARINE)

⅓ CUP PACKED DARK BROWN SUGAR

3 TABLESPOONS GRANULATED SUGAR

1 TEASPOON VANILLA EXTRACT

1¾ CUPS ALL-PURPOSE FLOUR

1 CUP PECANS (4 OUNCES), CHOPPED

1 Preheat oven to 350°F.

2 In large bowl, with mixer at medium-low speed, beat butter, brown and granulated sugars, and vanilla until creamy. Reduce speed to low and beat in flour until blended (dough will be crumbly). With wooden spoon, stir dough until it holds together.

3 Divide dough in half. Pat each dough half evenly onto bottom of two ungreased 8-inch round cake pans. Sprinkle with pecans; press lightly to make nuts stick.

4 Bake until lightly browned around edges and firm in center, 23 to 25 minutes, rotating pans between upper and lower oven racks halfway through baking. Transfer pans to wire racks. With small sharp knife, cut each round into 12 wedges.

5 Cool completely in pans on wire racks.

EACH COOKIE: ABOUT 130 CALORIES | 1G PROTEIN | 12G CARBOHYDRATE | 9G TOTAL FAT (4G SATURATED) | 0.5G FIBER | 16MG CHOLESTEROL | 60MG SODIUM

INDEX

PHOTOGRAPHY CREDITS

Sang An: 63, 136

Monica Buck: 78, 147

Squire Fox: 7

Brian Hagiwara: 9, 13 (top photos), 134

iStockphoto: Bryce Kroll: 13 bottom; Shanna Hendrickson: 49

Frances Janisch: 16, 54

Rita Maas: 51, 127

Steven Mark Needham: 8, 43, 52, 68, 84, 96, 103, 107 (both photos), 113, 117 (both photos), 120

Alan Richardson: 141, 169

Ann Stratton: 5, 15

Mark Thomas: 3, 21, 23, 27, 30, 45 (both photos), 46, 58, 77 (both photos), 125, 133, 145, 155, 163, 164, 167

FRONT COVER: Mark Thomas
SPINE: Mark Thomas
BACK COVER: (clockwise from top left): Steven Mark Needham, Mark Thomas, Steven Mark Needham

METRIC EQUIVALENTS

The recipes that appear in this cookbook use the standard United States method for measuring liquid and dry or solid ingredients (teaspoons, tablespoons, and cups). The information on this chart is provided to help cooks outside the U.S. successfully use these recipes. All equivalents are approximate.

METRIC EQUIVALENTS FOR DIFFERENT TYPES OF INGREDIENTS
A standard cup measure of a dry or solid ingredient will vary in weight depending on the type of ingredient. A standard cup of liquid is the same volume for any type of liquid. Use the following chart when converting standard cup measures to grams (weight) or milliliters (volume).

Standard Cup	Fine Powder (e.g. flour)	Grain (e.g. rice)	Granular (e.g. sugar)	Liquid Solids (e.g. butter)	Liquid (e.g. milk)
1	140 g	150 g	190 g	200 g	240 ml
¾	105 g	113 g	143 g	150 g	180 ml
⅔	93 g	100 g	125 g	133 g	160 ml
½	70 g	75 g	95 g	100 g	120 ml
⅓	47 g	50 g	63 g	67 g	80 ml
¼	35 g	38 g	48 g	50 g	60 ml
⅛	18 g	19 g	24 g	25 g	30 ml

USEFUL EQUIVALENTS FOR LIQUID INGREDIENTS BY VOLUME

¼ tsp=						1 ml
½ tsp=						2 ml
1 tsp =						5 ml
3 tsp =	1 tbls =			½ fl oz =		15 ml
	2 tbls =	⅛ cup =		1 fl oz =		30 ml
	4 tbls =	¼ cup =		2 fl oz =		60 ml
	5⅓ tbls =	⅓ cup =		3 fl oz =		80 ml
	8 tbls =	½ cup =		4 fl oz =		120 ml
	10⅔ tbls =	⅔ cup =		5 fl oz =		160 ml
	12 tbls =	¾ cup =		6 fl oz =		180 ml
	16 tbls =	1 cup =		8 fl oz =		240 ml
	1 pt =	2 cups =		16 fl oz =		480 ml
	1 qt =	4 cups =		32 fl oz =		960 ml
				33 fl oz	= 1000 ml	=1 L

USEFUL EQUIVALENTS FOR COOKING/OVEN TEMPERATURES

	Fahrenheit	Celsius	Gas Mark
Freeze Water	32° F	0° C	
Room Temperature	68° F	20° C	
Boil Water	212° F	100° C	
Bake	325° F	160° C	3
	350° F	180° C	4
	375° F	190° C	5
	400° F	200° C	6
	425° F	220° C	7
	450° F	230° C	8
Broil			Grill

USEFUL EQUIVALENTS FOR DRY INGREDIENTS BY WEIGHT
(To convert ounces to grams, multiply the number of ounces by 30.)

1 oz	=	¹⁄₁₆ lb	=	30 g
2 oz	=	¼ lb	=	120 g
4 oz	=	½ lb	=	240 g
8 oz	=	¾ lb	=	360 g
16 oz	=	1 lb	=	480 g

USEFUL EQUIVALENTS LENGTH
(To convert inches to centimeters, multiply the number of inches by 2.5.)

1 in	=		2.5 cm
6 in	= ½ ft =		15 cm
12 in	= 1 ft =		30 cm
36 in	= 3 ft = 1 yd	= 90 cm	
40 in	=		100 cm = 1 m

THE GOOD HOUSEKEEPING TRIPLE-TEST PROMISE

At *Good Housekeeping*, we want to make sure that every recipe we print works in any oven, with any brand of ingredient, no matter what. That's why, in our test kitchens at the **Good Housekeeping Research Institute**, we go all out: We test each recipe at least three times—and, often, several more times after that.

When a recipe is first developed, one member of our team prepares the dish and we judge it on these criteria: It must be **delicious, family-friendly, healthy**, and **easy to make**.

1. The recipe is then tested several more times to fine-tune the flavor and ease of preparation, always by the same team member, using the same equipment.

2. Next, another team member follows the recipe as written, **varying the brands of ingredients** and **kinds of equipment.** Even the types of stoves we use are changed.

3. A third team member repeats the whole process **using yet another set of equipment** and **alternative ingredients.**

By the time the recipes appear on these pages, they are guaranteed to work in any kitchen, including yours. WE PROMISE.